U.S.-Cuban Relations in the 21st Century:

A Follow-on Report

U.S.-Cuban Relations in the 21st Century

*A Follow-on Chairman's Report
of an Independent Task Force
Sponsored by the
Council on Foreign Relations*

Bernard W. Aronson and William D. Rogers,
Co-Chairs

Julia Sweig and Walter Mead,
Project Directors

The Council on Foreign Relations, Inc., a nonprofit, nonpartisan national organization founded in 1921, is dedicated to promoting understanding of international affairs through the free and civil exchange of ideas. The Council's members are dedicated to the belief that America's peace and prosperity are firmly linked to that of the world. From this flows the mission of the Council: to foster America's understanding of other nations—their peoples, cultures, histories, hopes, quarrels, and ambitions—and thus to serve our nation through study and debate, private and public.

THE COUNCIL TAKES NO INSTITUTIONAL POSITION ON POLICY ISSUES AND HAS NO AFFILIATION WITH THE U.S. GOVERNMENT. ALL STATEMENTS OF FACT AND EXPRESSIONS OF OPINION CONTAINED IN ALL ITS PUBLICATIONS ARE THE SOLE RESPONSIBILITY OF THE AUTHOR OR AUTHORS.

The Council will sponsor an Independent Task Force when (1) an issue of current and critical importance to U.S. foreign policy arises, and (2) it seems that a group diverse in backgrounds and perspectives may, nonetheless, be able to reach a meaningful consensus on a policy through private and nonpartisan deliberations. Typically, a Task Force meets between two and five times over a brief period to ensure the relevance of its work.

Upon reaching a conclusion, a Task Force issues a report, and the Council publishes its text and posts it on the Council website. Task Force Reports can take three forms: (1) a strong and meaningful policy consensus, with Task Force members endorsing the general policy thrust and judgments reached by the group, though not necessarily every finding and recommendation; (2) a report stating the various policy positions, each as sharply and fairly as possible; or (3) a "Chairman's Report," where Task Force members who agree with the Chairman's Report may associate themselves with it, while those who disagree may submit dissenting statements. Upon reaching a conclusion, a Task Force may also ask individuals who were not members of the Task Force to associate themselves with the Task Force Report to enhance its impact. All Task Force Reports "benchmark" their findings against current administration policy in order to make explicit areas of agreement and disagreement. The Task Force is solely responsible for its report. The Council takes no institutional position.

For further information about the Council or this Task Force, please write the Council on Foreign Relations, 58 East 68th Street, New York, NY 10021, or call the Director of Communications at (212) 434-9400. Visit our website at www.cfr.org.

CONTENTS

FOREWORD

In 1998 the Council on Foreign Relations sponsored an Independent Task Force on U.S.-Cuban Relations in the 21st Century. Chaired by two former assistant secretaries of state for inter-American affairs, Bernard W. Aronson and William D. Rogers, the Task Force made recommendations for U.S. policy toward Cuba in light of the end of the Cold War and the inevitable transition to come on the island. Immediately after the Task Force completed its deliberations, the Clinton administration adopted a number of policy measures recommended by the Task Force, in particular those that would increase people-to-people contacts between Americans and Cubans.

After publishing the first report, I asked the co-chairs to continue the Task Force on a stand-by basis and invited several new members to join. The Task Force convened on several occasions during the ensuing two years to review developments in bilateral relations and on the ground in Cuba. The Task Force now includes widely respected scholars, lawyers, businesspeople, labor leaders, and former government officials representing a broad range of views and backgrounds. A number of congressional, State Department, and White House staff members participated in Task Force meetings as observers. In addition, under William Rogers's leadership, the Task Force staff conducted research and consulted with a group of experts to review and compare property expropriations and to consider alternatives for property-claims settlements in Cuba.

At the same time, the policy community, Congress, and the public have been engaged in an evolving debate over the appropriate course for beginning engagement with the Cuban people and preparing for and facilitating a peaceful transition on the island. This debate has focused largely on U.S. agricultural and medical exports and on American travel to Cuba. In July 2000 the House and Senate voted to end sanctions on food and medical sales to Cuba. The House also voted in favor of a measure that would, in effect, end the travel ban. But the Trade Sanctions Reform and Export Enhancement Act passed by Congress and signed by the president contains prohibitions that, by barring U.S. commercial financing, will virtually proscribe food sales to Cuba. And by codifying travel regulations, the new law stands to dampen the possibility for the executive branch to expand people-to-people initiatives, if President George W. Bush so desires.

For the purposes of considering the new chairman's report, the Task Force met on two occasions in the fall of 2000. In addition to the members and observers of the Task Force, the group sought comments and input from a wide variety of individuals, holding meetings in Minneapolis, Miami, and Houston. As in the endeavor that produced the first report, the Task Force continued to explore pragmatic policy measures toward Cuba based on the conditions shaping the bilateral relationship, domestic Cuban developments, and the evolving debate in the United States. In the first report, most of the recommendations called for presidential action rather than new legislation. The Task Force continues to recognize that, despite recent changes in the law, the president retains broad authority to modify policy toward Cuba. But in light of recent congressional engagement, many of the recommendations in this follow-on report can be implemented either by the executive branch or through legislative change. In both cases, the Task Force favors a bipartisan policy toward Cuba and, moreover, demonstrates that such an approach is indeed possible.

In this follow-on report, the Task Force again demonstrates that the U.S. government can take many useful steps short of lifting economic sanctions and restoring diplomatic relations. Indeed, this report moves beyond recent congressional action in several important respects by recommending, for example: selling agricultural and medical products with commercial U.S. financing, though not government credits; travel to Cuba by all Americans; direct commercial flights and ferry services; environmental and conservation cooperation; continued counternarcotics cooperation and low- and mid-level exchanges between the U.S. and Cuban military forces; working with Cuba to support the Colombian peace process; limited American investment to support the Cuban private sector and capture the market generated by increased American travel to Cuba; actively promoting international labor standards in Cuba; resolving expropriation claims by licensing American claimants to negotiate settlements directly with Cuba, including in the form of direct joint venture investments; and supporting Cuban observer status in the International Monetary Fund, World Bank, and Inter-American Development Bank.

I would like to extend my thanks again to Bernard Aronson and William Rogers, the co-chairs of the Task Force, for their commitment and leadership; to Julia Sweig and Walter Mead, the project directors, for their excellent work; and to Council members and others around the country for their input and perspective. Finally, the Task Force members themselves deserve my sincere thanks for lending their time, intelligence, and integrity to this important issue.

Leslie H. Gelb
President
Council on Foreign Relations

ACKNOWLEDGMENTS

The Independent Task Force on U.S.-Cuban Relations in the 21st Century sponsored by the Council on Foreign Relations has benefited from the assistance of many individuals. For two years now, we have worked under the intellectual leadership provided by the Task Force co-chairs, Bernard W. Aronson and William D. Rogers. We are also indebted to the members and observers of the Task Force, whose experience and knowledge contributed substantially to the success of this report.

The Task Force also benefited from discussions held through the Council's National Program with the James A. Baker III Institute for Public Policy of Rice University in Houston, the Dante B. Fascell North-South Center at the University of Miami, and the Hubert H. Humphrey Institute of Public Affairs of the University of Minnesota. Many of the comments we received in these sessions helped shaped the final report, and we are grateful for the candor and wisdom we found outside of our habitual Washington–New York enclave.

At the Council on Foreign Relations we would like to acknowledge the support for the Task Force provided by Council President Leslie H. Gelb, Senior Vice President Michael Peters, Vice President Janice Murray, Director of Publishing Patricia Dorff, Communications Director April Palmerlee, and National Program Deputy Director Irina Faskianos. Our colleagues on the Task Force staff, specifically Research Associate Jessica Duda and Program Associate Meghan Bishop, provided expert research and administrative support without which this report could not have been produced.

Finally, we are grateful to the John D. & Catherine T. MacArthur Foundation, the General Services Foundation, and the Christopher Reynolds Foundation for the financial support each provided for the work of this Task Force.

Julia Sweig
Walter Mead
Project Directors
Council on Foreign Relations

INTRODUCTION

In the last quarter of 1998, following the visit to Cuba of Pope John Paul II, the Council on Foreign Relations convened an Independent Task Force to assess U.S. policy toward Cuba in the post–Cold War era. The Task Force represents a bipartisan group of former State Department officials, congressional staff, labor leaders, and students of Latin American affairs and U.S. foreign policy from a cross section of think tanks, academic and religious institutions, businesses, trade unions, and government agencies. In a chairman's report issued in January 1999, the Task Force recommended a number of steps to strengthen civil society in Cuba, expand people-to-people contact between Cubans and Americans, and "contribute to rapid, peaceful, democratic transition in Cuba while safeguarding the vital interests of the United States."[1]

Three key assumptions guided the Task Force in its efforts to develop a bipartisan consensus, spanning the liberal-conservative spectrum, for changes in U.S. policy toward Cuba. First, we agreed that the United States should set its sights beyond President Fidel Castro and focus on how to build bridges between the American and Cuban people. Second, we determined not to recreate the continuing public debate over whether to tighten or lift the embargo. Instead, with rare exceptions, we have proposed new policy measures that could be implemented within the framework of current law through regulations authorized by the president. Finally, we determined that no change in policy should have the primary effect of consolidating, or appearing to legitimize, the political status quo on the island.

Our first set of recommendations therefore focused on family reunification, people-to-people contacts, humanitarian aid, the

---

[1] *U.S.-Cuban Relations in the 21st Century: Report of an Independent Task Force Sponsored by the Council on Foreign Relations* (New York: Council on Foreign Relations, January 1999), p. 10.

private sector, and the national interest. Among the measures we proposed were: to lift restrictions on travel by Cuban Americans to Cuba and on the amount of remittances family members can send to the island; allow Cuban Americans to claim tax exemptions for dependents living in Cuba; lift most restrictions on the sale of food and medicine to Cuba; allow increased travel to Cuba for research, scientific, cultural, religious, educational, humanitarian, and athletic purposes, as well as commercial flights; ease restrictions on travel to the United States by Cuban academics, artists, athletes, and mid-level officials; open limited American commercial activity on the island; probe possibilities for counternarcotics cooperation; and consider military-to-military confidence-building measures.[2]

SUBSEQUENT POLICY CHANGES

Shortly after we concluded our work, the Clinton administration announced a series of measures that, though more limited in scope than those we had urged, were consistent with the spirit of our recommendations and, in the case of people-to-people exchanges, adopted certain of the Task Force's recommendations. In making these announcements, the White House noted that a number of additional measures contained in our report would remain under active consideration for future implementation.

The most significant of the administration's January 1999 steps were designed to allow greater people-to-people contact. These changes included substantially expanding legal, licensed travel for Americans wishing to visit the island, streamlining the temporary visa process for Cuban professionals who wish to visit this country, and allowing charter flights to Cuba to depart from Los Angeles and New York as well as Miami, to Havana and other cities in Cuba. Other measures proposed by the Clinton administration would begin direct mail service between the two countries as authorized by the 1992 Cuban Democracy Act,

---

[2]See recommendations from our 1999 Task Force Report, which are excerpted in the Appendix.

increase funding for Radio and TV Martí, and promote public diplomacy to call attention to human rights abuses.

In light of a broader congressional debate over sanctions policy, particularly regarding food and medicine trade bans, the Clinton administration indicated it would streamline the licensing of medical sales to Cuba and license the sale of food and agricultural inputs to nongovernmental entities on the island.

In addition, the administration proposed to Cuba a series of steps designed to enhance counternarcotics cooperation. Direct bilateral talks in 1999 resulted in the stationing of a U.S. Coast Guard official in March 2000 at the U.S. Interests Section in Havana, as a liaison to search vessels for contraband. The two countries also upgraded their communications regarding counternarcotics from fax to phone.

In addition to these measures that echoed our earlier report's proposals, last year the U.S. Department of State announced that it found no evidence to support including Cuba on the annually updated "majors list" of countries that the U.S. government determines are involved in illicit drug production and transit, and are therefore eligible for U.S. government assistance only if certified by the president.

AN OPPORTUNITY FOR A FOLLOW-ON REPORT

Since early 1999, congressional and public debates over U.S. policy toward Cuba have continued to evolve, suggesting that the desire within our Task Force to reach a new bipartisan consensus on Cuba policy is shared by the wider community.

In March 2000, Senate Foreign Relations Committee Chairman Jesse Helms (R-N.C.) included in an authorizations bill an amendment ending sanctions on the sale of food and medicine to Cuba. This bill passed by voice vote in the full committee. Similar votes in the Senate and House followed last summer, as well as a vote in the House to lift—or, more precisely, not to enforce—the travel ban. Simultaneously, the congressional vote in favor of Permanent Normal Trade Relations (PNTR) for

China helped strengthen the consensus for engagement, as opposed to isolation, as the primary policy option for promoting economic and political freedom.

In addition, the new people-to-people measures successfully facilitated bridge-building across a broad spectrum of arenas, including the humanitarian, religious, cultural, athletic, academic, public health, environmental, and scientific fields. In 1999 an estimated 150,000 to 200,000 Americans traveled to Cuba, up from fewer than 40,000 in 1998. Likewise, the number of Cubans visiting the United States on temporary visas increased substantially—to 40,000 in 1999 from 9,000 in 1998. The year 2000 will have recorded even greater two-way travel.

None of this, however, has led to a loosening of Cuban policy toward dissidents or improvements in human rights. Cuba remains a one-party state that seeks to suppress any independent political activity. In 1999 the Cuban National Assembly passed laws that criminalized transmitting to foreigners economic and foreign investment information related to the enforcement of the U.S. Helms-Burton Act of 1996, and Cuban intellectuals are experiencing intensified pressures for conformity. Although international human rights groups and activists on the ground in Cuba report a reduced number of political prisoners—between 300 and 350—they also note that extended jail-time is now reserved for high-profile dissidents, while lesser-known activists face harassment, house arrest, or temporary detentions. The government has failed to make good on its promise of allowing greater freedom for the Catholic Church. Both dissident activity and repression of dissident activity continue.[3] Periodic expulsions of journalists and others who attempt to support the dissident movement in Cuba continue. And the Inter American Press Association recently noted that "faced with harassment and persecution, more than 20 independent journalists have been forced to go into

---

[3] "Cuba Short Term Detention and Harassment of Dissidents," Amnesty International Report AMR 25/04/00 (New York: Amnesty International, March 30, 2000), p. 2.

exile over the past six months," condemning "Havana's totalitarian regime."[4]

Nevertheless, we have been heartened by the fact that the international community has begun to focus greater attention on human rights on the island and on the importance of promoting a peaceful, democratic transition and defending human rights in Cuba. When King Juan Carlos II of Spain joined Spanish Prime Minister José María Aznar and such Latin American heads of state as Mexican President Ernesto Zedillo at the November 1999 Ibero-American Summit in Havana, they and other Latin American heads of state pointedly sought meetings with prominent dissidents, including veteran human rights activists Elizardo Sánchez and Gustavo Arcos and independent journalist Raúl Rivero. These leaders also spoke publicly and critically about the lack of democracy in Cuba.

Moreover, in April 2000 at the U.N. Human Rights Commission meeting in Geneva, several Latin American and European countries that each year previously had voted against the U.S. embargo at the U.N. General Assembly either voted for or abstained from a resolution condemning human rights practices in Cuba, which passed by a vote of 21 to 18 with 14 abstentions.[5] The vote prompted Cuba to withdraw its application for membership in the post-Lomé accord for trade with the European Union and to opt instead for bilateral aid relationships.

In light of these developments and the change in the U.S. administration in January 2001, the Task Force decided to issue a follow-on report. We do so because we continue to believe that we

---

[4]Inter American Press Association General Assembly Declaration, Santiago, Chile, October 2000.

[5]*In favor:* Argentina, Canada, Chile, Czech Republic, El Salvador, France, Germany, Guatemala, Italy, Japan, Latvia, Luxembourg, Morocco, Norway, Poland, Portugal, Republic of Korea, Romania, Spain, United Kingdom of Great Britain and Northern Ireland, United States of America. *Against:* Bhutan, Burundi, China, Cuba, India, Indonesia, Liberia, Madagascar, Niger, Nigeria, Pakistan, Peru, Republic of Congo, Russian Federation, Sudan, Tunisia, Venezuela, Zambia. *Abstaining:* Bangladesh, Botswana, Brazil, Colombia, Ecuador, Mauritius, Mexico, Nepal, Philippines, Qatar, Rwanda, Senegal, Sri Lanka, Switzerland. See, United Nations, "Commission on Human Rights Report on the Fifty-Sixth session Part II, 20 March–28 April 2000" (July 21, 2000), pp. 60–61.

are in a new era and a new environment that require the United States to rethink its policy toward Cuba. We say this for a number of reasons.

First, the Cold War has ended. The former Soviet Union—once Cuba's chief military, economic, and ideological supporter—has disappeared. The east European nations once under Soviet domination, with which Cuba had close supportive relations, are now among the most forthright critics of Cuba's suppression of human rights. In nations throughout the Western Hemisphere, the democratic ideal has triumphed. Despite continued challenges and setbacks, electoral democracy is widely considered to be the only legitimate form of government in the Western Hemisphere; no serious observer believes that the Cuban political model represents the wave of the future. Although authoritarian tendencies and flawed elections continue to challenge the Americas, Cuba remains isolated as the only nation in the Western Hemisphere in which the head of state rules without having been subject to competitive elections.

On the economic front as well, the closed, statist economic model has collapsed in nation after nation. The future clearly belongs to open economies that can integrate with global finance, trade, and investment. Although there is a vigorous debate in the Western Hemisphere and worldwide about the best way to marry open markets with economic equity, no serious observer believes that the closed economic model represented by Cuba will survive. Indeed, the loss of Soviet bloc subsidies and the pressures of the global marketplace have forced Cuba to legalize the dollar, seek joint ventures with foreign partners, accept labor dislocation in its domestic economy, and allow private economic activity to begin.

Echoing our first report, the primary and overriding objective of the United States—containing the spread of Cuban communism in this hemisphere—has been achieved. We believe that whatever shape it may take, Cuban-style communism will not long survive the post-Castro era in Cuba. Indeed, we believe that many Cubans, including perhaps many who hold official positions, understand that a transition to a democratic and free-market Cuba is inevitable.

For all these reasons, we therefore continue to believe that the United States can discuss policy toward Cuba with confidence and from a position of strength. Cuba's official rhetoric remains antithetical to American values, but we note that in a 1998 report cleared by the entire U.S. intelligence community, the Defense Intelligence Agency concluded that "at present, Cuba does not pose a significant military threat to the United States or to other countries in the region."[6] We note also that whether from conviction or from necessity imposed by the loss of military and economic assistance from the former Soviet Union, Cuba has publicly renounced its former policy of material support for violent revolutionary movements. We are heartened by the east Europeans' success in replacing communist dictatorships with democratic societies and note the important role that civil society played in these successful transitions. We recognize that Cuba is in many respects different from these east European examples, and that civil society remains effectively repressed and suppressed. However, we nevertheless continue to believe that engagement with ordinary Cubans, and also with those mid-level officials who recognize that a transition is coming, can help promote the emergence of civil society and a more rapid, peaceful transition to democracy on the island.

We are aware, however, that past political instability in Cuba has repeatedly created pressures for U.S. intervention on and around the island. Many future scenarios could unleash these types of pressures on the United States. Should a successor government emerge in the wake of Fidel Castro's death or incapacity, for example, it is unlikely to command the same authority as the current government. Indeed, such a government might feel the need to demonstrate its control early in its tenure at the same time as Cuban citizens might be tempted to test its perceived weakness.

---

[6]Defense Intelligence Agency, "The Cuban Threat to U.S. National Security," April 22, 1998. The DIA coordinated with the National Intelligence Council, the Central Intelligence Agency, the National Security Agency, and the Intelligence and Research Bureau at the State Department.

There are many possible future scenarios that could lead to pressures for the United States to intervene militarily. Thousands of Cubans might seek to flee the island and a successor regime might use force to try to stop them. Also, civil unrest could break out for a variety of reasons, and one branch of the armed forces might be reluctant to use violence against its citizens. If, under any of the above scenarios, thousands of Cubans set out in rafts and makeshift vessels for the United States, their relatives and friends in Florida would likely head to sea to rescue them, as occurred in the Mariel Harbor boatlift of 1980. Fighting on the island could also break out and involve U.S.-based Cuban citizens or Cuban Americans who would find it difficult to stand by while their relatives were under attack or they perceived their homeland might be liberated. We hope none of these scenarios unfolds, but policymakers must be prepared for the worst case and not merely hope that such developments will not occur on their watch.

We believe that the recommendations we have prepared may well enhance the prospects for a nonviolent and democratic political process in Cuba and lessen the likelihood of confrontation and conflict that might inspire calls for American intervention. By issuing these recommendations, we are not predicting violence in Cuba's future. We continue to believe that a rapid, peaceful transition to democratic government is what the Cuban people want—it is certainly what we hope will transpire. Nevertheless, we believe that the United States should now adopt a series of measures that may reduce the chances of U.S. military involvement, should Cuba's transition go awry, and by doing so, make Cuba's peaceful transition to democracy more likely.

We note, also, that in the wake of the divisions generated by the case of Elián González, relations between U.S. federal authorities and the Cuban-American community have been damaged and frayed by distrust, anger, bitterness, and recriminations. Whatever one believes about the merits of that case, the new administration in Washington should make a major, sustained effort to rebuild communication and trust with Cuban Americans. Several of our recommendations are directed to that end. We believe that a trusting working relationship between the federal government and the Cuban-American community is crucial for managing potential future crises on the island.

Our recommendations in this second report also attempt to confront and resolve some of the most intractable problems that a successor, democratic government in Cuba might inherit. We have learned from watching the transitions from communist dictatorships and command economies in other nations—whether Nicaragua or the states of the former Soviet Union—that even after electoral democracy triumphs, the burden of the past weighs heavily on a nation's capacity to recover, particularly economically. In Nicaragua, for example, sorting out competing property claims posed a major obstacle to economic growth and foreign investment for the new democratic government in 1991 and remains an irritant in U.S.-Nicaraguan bilateral relations. We also know that the failure of new democracies to grow and prosper can relegitimize anti-democratic forces and threaten a return to authoritarian policies—a danger that has hovered over post-communist Russia. With regard to Cuba, we believe it is both important and possible for the United States to begin to identify issues, such as outstanding U.S. property claims and labor rights, that can be addressed now rather than leave them as an albatross around the neck of a successor, democratic government.

We thus have sought to identify such problems, as well as the prospects for current and future American investment and trade, which may be addressed prior to a transition. Our hope in doing so is to help ease the difficulties of a transition democratic government and reduce the obstacles to rapid economic recovery and growth.

SUMMARY AND FRAMEWORK OF
RECOMMENDATIONS

Two years ago we began our recommendations with a statement of basic principles. That statement remains relevant today and continues to guide our approach.[7] We then made a basic decision that our Task Force would not join the protracted public debate over whether the United States should unilaterally lift its embargo. That is still the case today, especially since we continue to believe—as our first report demonstrated—that there indeed exists significant common ground for advancing U.S. policy toward Cuba in other ways.

Our new set of recommendations builds on the first set; in some cases, it goes beyond them. For example, the first set contained recommendations almost entirely directed toward the executive branch. To be sure, some of the Task Force members felt that any executive action taken toward Cuba should fully reflect the views of Congress, and some Task Force members dissented from certain of the first report's recommendations. Given the extent of the subsequent debate in Congress, we felt it was appropriate for this follow-on report to make some recommendations that Congress may consider as well.

Our recommendations seek to build and strengthen bridges between the Cuban and American people, promote family reunification, address current and future matters of U.S. national security, promote labor rights and facilitate resolution of prop-

---

[7]Our 1999 report was guided by this basic statement of principle: "No change in U.S. policy toward Cuba should have the primary effect of consolidating or legitimizing the status quo on the island. On the other hand, every aspect of U.S. foreign and economic policy toward Cuba should be judged by a very pragmatic standard: whether it contributes to rapid, peaceful, democratic change in Cuba while safeguarding the vital interests of the United States." *U.S.-Cuban Relations in the 21st Century: Report of an Independent Task Force Sponsored by the Council on Foreign Relations*, p. 10.

erty claims, and further expose Cuba to international norms and practices.

We note that in the final days of the 106th Congress, the House and Senate voted to approve an agricultural appropriations bill containing an amendment to remove food and medicine from unilateral sanctions. We find two provisions of the new law troubling, one regarding export sanctions and the other regarding travel. First, the amendment grants the president the authority to allow the sale of food and medicine to each of the countries on the State Department's terrorist list—Sudan, Libya, North Korea, Iran, and Cuba—under a one-year general license. However, only with respect to Cuba does the new law prohibit U.S. banks from providing private commercial financing for such sales—the amendment permits only third-country financing. This provision was set into law despite two previous votes in the Senate and one in the House, which called for an end to agricultural and medical sanctions on Cuba without restrictions on private U.S. financing.

The second provision of the new law relates to travel by American citizens to Cuba. It was included without public hearing on the matter and despite a vote in the House of Representatives, by a margin of 232-186, to lift the travel ban indirectly by withholding the funds necessary to enforce current restrictions. The new provision codifies into law 12 existing categories of legal travel, currently set forth in the Cuban Assets Control Regulations, that can be licensed under specific or general licenses. At the same time, it creates an additional category for specifically licensed travel to Cuba by potential American agricultural vendors. The new provision states that all travel to Cuba outside of the existing categories will be considered "tourism." And "tourism," under the new law, is explicitly prohibited.

The travel categories codified by the legislation—trips by journalists, government officials, Cuban Americans, and professional researchers, as well as for religious, academic, athletic, informational, artistic, and humanitarian exchanges—exclude an additional category that heretofore gave the Office of Foreign Assets Control (OFAC) discretionary authority to issue licenses for the purpose of travel not specifically covered by the other 12 categories. Under a strict interpretation of the new provision, many commonsense matters that require travel to Cuba—for example, morale-related visits by friends and family to U.S. officials based there, a Medevac helicopter to provide emergency care for American citizens, travel by authorized travel-service operators such as airline charter companies, and also federal prosecutors and private defense attorneys to take testimony in Cuba (in espionage cases, for example)—could be prohibited. And although at the time this report was issued it was too early to determine definitively the chilling effect of this new legislation, we have learned from one president of a major travel agency licensed by the administration to provide charter flights that these provisions, now the law of the land, would bar the managers of licensed travel-service providers from traveling to Cuba to arrange future licensed travel. In addition, as President Clinton noted, the law will certainly constrain the American president's ability to pursue creative people-to-people initiatives and will dampen efforts by Cuban Americans to maintain the family ties they choose to have with their relatives on the island.

We note below the extent to which these new provisions of law affect our recommendations regarding family reunification, agricultural and medical exports, and travel.

RECOMMENDATIONS

BASKET ONE: FAMILY REUNIFICATION AND MIGRATION

Over the last 41 years, political persecution and exile, as well as the hostile division between our two countries, have forcibly kept Cubans and their loved ones apart—sometimes for decades, sometimes forever. The publicity over Elián González, the six-year-old Cuban boy found clinging to an inner tube off the coast of Florida in November 1999, alerted many Americans to the human dimensions of this tragedy. Like thousands of other Cuban citizens, Elián's mother trusted her own life and that of her son to an ill-fated voyage on the open sea. Elián's survival caught the world's attention. Since 1959, some 200,000 Cubans have crossed the Florida Strait on inner tubes, rafts, and boats; 600,000 have fled by plane. In the early 1960s, many Cuban parents became desperate enough to send their children to the United States under the Catholic Church's Operation Pedro Pan, so that their children might grow up in a free society. One of these children is now a member of our Task Force.

We believe that for humanitarian reasons as well as for the national interest and security of the United States, U.S. policymakers should take all possible steps to remove the obstacles that divide Cuban Americans from their family members in Cuba and promote lawful family reunification. In making these recommendations, our Task Force wrestled with the moral dilemma posed by the practice of returning Cubans to the island. Some on our Task Force felt that Cuba should be considered a special case, and that as long as a closed, repressive system persists on the island, the United States has a moral obligation to accept anyone attempting to flee, whatever his or her motive or circumstance. On the other hand, a special policy of open borders for all Cubans encourages people to take to the sea and tempt death. We do not want to legitimize the dangerous practice of alien smuggling, either from Cuba or from any other country in the world. That is why the recommendations in this section, taken together, attempt to maximize the opportunity for family reunification and safe, legal migration to the United States.

1. *End Restrictions on Family Visits.* At present, the United States permits Cuban Americans to travel only once per year to Cuba without first asking permission, and then only for a humanitarian emergency. We recommend an end to all restrictions on visits by Cuban Americans to Cuba. Since current travel regulations do grant Cuban Americans a general license for travel once annually, we propose that the president eliminate the once-per-year limitation and permit Cuban Americans to travel under a general license as often as they like—the same rights currently accorded to professional researchers and full-time journalists. The federal government should not be the judge of how often Cuban Americans—or any other Americans—need to visit relatives living abroad. Nor should existing or forthcoming regulations and laws force Cuban Americans to violate the law in order to see their family members, for whatever purpose they deem fit.

2. *Lift the Ceiling on Remittances.* Current regulations permit all American citizens to send $1,200 per year to any Cuban family other than those of high-ranking government officials. Indeed, an estimated $500 to $800 million in annual remittances—sent mainly by Cuban Americans—give a lifeline to hundreds of thousands of Cuban citizens, provide them with a modicum of independence from the Cuban state, and support the creation and growth of small businesses. We recommend eliminating the ceiling so that personal decisions and financial resources, rather than government regulations, determine how much financial support Americans can provide to their Cuban families.

3. *Allow Cuban Americans to Claim Relatives as Dependents.* Currently, American citizens with dependent relatives living in Canada and Mexico can claim them as dependents for federal income tax purposes, provided they meet the other relevant U.S. Internal Revenue Service (IRS) requirements. As in our first report, we recommend an amendment to U.S. tax laws so that American taxpayers with dependents who are residents of Cuba can also claim this deduction. Moreover, we recommend that the same rights be extended to taxpayers of other national origins who have dependents in their home countries, if they meet the other relevant IRS requirements.

4. *Allow Retirement to Cuba for Cuban Americans.* As we suggested in our first report, we recommend that retired and/or disabled Cuban Americans be allowed to return to Cuba if they choose, collecting Social Security, Medicare, and other pension benefits to which they are entitled in the United States, and be accorded corresponding banking facilities, as is the principle with respect to other countries.

5. *Revise Criteria for Temporary Visas.* The United States should do more to facilitate visits by Cuban citizens to see their relatives in the United States. Current policy on temporary visas treats Cuban applicants like it treats those from other foreign countries, applying a selection of high criteria such as salary, types of bank accounts, age, or property ownership to estimate their likelihood of returning home voluntarily. The nature of the Cuban government and economy makes these standards not only prohibitive but inappropriate for Cuban applicants. Moreover, recent spot checks by the U.S. Interests Section in Havana have found a surprisingly high rate of return to the island among those who visit the United States, a finding that should ease the anxiety of consular officials who are concerned that temporary visitors from poor countries will not abide by the terms of their visas. Although we do not minimize the task of adopting new criteria for Cuba, we believe that it should be done and that Cuban applications that meet these criteria should be processed as quickly and favorably as pos-

sible, provided the applicants have letters of invitation from relatives in the United States. We recommend also that visas should be granted for a longer period of time than the customary thirty-day allotment and that the appropriate visas be granted to Cuban nationals visiting the United States for fellowships and study. We note that in the last year the number of Cubans visiting the United States on temporary visas has increased more than four-fold, to 40,000 in 1999 from 9,000 in 1998. We applaud this development and hope the issuance of temporary visas—a practice that allows Cubans to develop their own, independent views of American society—continues to increase. We recognize as well that unnecessary impediments, such as bureaucratic obstacles and exorbitant fees erected by the Cuban authorities, prevent many Cuban citizens from taking advantage of visa opportunities to travel to the United States. We call upon the Cuban authorities to remove these barriers.

6. *Public Education to Accelerate Safe, Legal, and Orderly Family Reunification.* Cubans can currently pursue four programs to migrate legally to the United States: the immigrant visa program; the Special Program for Cuban Migrants, known as the "lottery system"; the program for political asylum seekers; and the worldwide lottery system. The most widely known is the "lottery system"; established following the 1994 migration accords, under which the United States agreed "that total legal migration to the United States from Cuba will be a minimum of 20,000 Cubans each year, not including immediate relatives of United States citizens." Several thousand more slots are potentially available in addition to the annual 20,000, which is the figure incorrectly and widely assumed to be the maximum available amount. For example, many of the 1.4 million people of Cuban origin living in the United States (including the 125,000 who have come since 1994) are not aware that they may acquire permanent residence status that would make their immediate relatives—children, spouses, and parents—eligible to apply for immigrant visas. We therefore recommend

that the U.S. Immigration and Naturalization Service (INS) and State Department, together with local authorities and community organizations, intensify public education efforts to inform Cuban-American residents of the legal mechanisms they may exercise. This way, their immediate relatives wishing to migrate may obtain immigrant visas, a category of legal migration that the United States makes available over and above the 20,000 visas distributed each year, mostly to winners of the "lottery." Moreover, we strongly encourage the Cuban government to permit radio, television, and the print media to transmit this information regarding legal options for migration to the United States to the Cuban people, and also to disseminate this information widely itself. Though participating in the "lottery" or waiting for an immigrant visa may extend the period of time Cubans must wait to enter the United States legally, we believe that taking advantage of the enhanced opportunities for legal migration is an important step toward reducing the life-threatening dangers of efforts to leave Cuba irregularly. If funds for a public information–community outreach program are currently not available in relevant agency budgets, Congress should make such an appropriation.

7. *Expand Consular Services.* Since our first report was issued, the demands on the U.S. Interests Section in Cuba have increased greatly. Current U.S. consular services in Cuba should not be limited to Havana. To process an increased number of legal Cuban migrants, we recommend that the United States open a subsection of its Havana consular office in Santiago de Cuba, a step that will also help the United States to fill the annual quota of several thousand slots available for political asylum seekers and to better monitor the treatment of Cubans returned to the island under the migration accords. Moreover, we recommend that the United States negotiate a reciprocal agreement with Cuba that will allow each country to expand its consular services—perhaps with Cuba opening a subsection of its current consulate in another U.S. city—to accommodate increased contact between citizens of both countries.

8. *Prosecute Alien Smugglers.* In spite of expanded opportunities for legal migration, there has been a troubling increase in alien smuggling from Cuba to the United States—a dangerous practice in which smugglers extract exorbitant fees for the perilous journey across the Florida Strait. The September 9, 1994, Joint Communiqué on U.S.-Cuba Immigration Agreement states that the United States and Cuba "reaffirm their support for the recently adopted U.N. General Assembly resolution on alien smuggling," and "pledged their cooperation to take prompt and effective action to prevent the transport of persons to the United States illegally." The communiqué also notes that "the United States has discontinued its practice of granting parole to all Cuban migrants who reach U.S. territory in irregular ways. The Republic of Cuba will take effective measures in every way it possibly can to prevent unsafe departures using mainly persuasive methods."

   Adherence by both Cuba and the United States to the 1994–95 migration agreements (the fundamental objectives of which are to prevent the loss of life and to safeguard American borders) requires the United States to prosecute smugglers. Family reunification measures—combined with a review of current automatic parole practices and criteria, including the existence of prior criminal records, and a more judicious application of the 1966 Cuban Adjustment Act—will, in our view, reduce the risk to life that so many Cubans are now undertaking while enhancing their opportunities to migrate to the United States legally and safely.

9. *Confront Neglected Immigration Issues.* A number of migration-related technical issues, such as fee structures and the timeliness and prohibitions of exit and entry-paper issuance for temporary and permanent migration, require more regular and serious communication. We believe such contact can increase the expanded opportunities for safe, orderly, and legal family reunification and is in the interest of both the Cuban people and the United States. Therefore, we recommend more regular, routine, and substantive contact through the Interests Sections

in both capitals. We also hope that the governments of both Cuba and the United States will seriously address the issues that each would bring to the table during such talks. These talks would provide the opportunity to revisit a stalled 1996 U.S. initiative proposing a return agreement with Cuba to repatriate, in a mutually acceptable, timely fashion, those with criminal records who are not already included on the list of "excludables" agreed to under the 1984 migration agreement.

BASKET TWO: INCREASING THE FREE FLOW OF IDEAS

In our first report we noted that expanding human contact to help spread information, new ideas, and fresh perspectives can help break the isolation of, and expand engagement in, Cuba. We recommended more licensed travel not only by individuals, but also by nongovernmental organizations (NGOs). As a result of the adoption of these recommendations, new bridges between the American and Cuban people now exist.

We also continue to believe that—as we have seen in successful transitions from communism to democracy in nations such as Poland, Nicaragua, and the former Soviet Union—often some officials in the old regime, because of long-standing conviction, a change of view, or a desire to adapt to changing political realities, can help the peaceful establishment of a new democratic polity.

The Task Force wrestled with the issue of lifting the ban on travel. Many members were concerned that this travel would largely be of a "tourist" nature, and that the proceeds would go to the Cuban government through its joint ventures with foreign hotel concerns, and thus strengthen its repressive capacities. Others noted, however, that no apparent weakening of the instruments of official repression was evident when Cuban state income was more constrained in the early 1990s. Still others argued that allowing unlimited travel by Cuban Americans to the island, as we propose, but not by all Americans, as we also propose, raises serious constitutional questions about whether such a distinction is warranted. Moreover, the large increase in people-to-people contacts proposed in our first report and implemented by the Clinton administration has already significantly increased the number of Americans staying on the island, many of whom, no doubt by necessity, stay in joint-venture tourist hotels. However, we also note that in many regions of Cuba, small, privately run restaurants, bed and breakfasts, and informal taxi and guide services are springing up—they benefit from this increased travel outside the confines of state authority.

On balance, the Task Force believes that freedom is contagious and that people-to-people contacts with ordinary American citizens will help convey democratic and free-market ideas to ordinary Cubans, while continuing to dispel the Cuban government's propaganda about the American government's hostility toward Cuba. We believe that when possible, in providing normal travel guidance about Cuba to visiting Americans, the State Department should highlight the availability of informal and private services in Cuba and note that the proceeds from such services benefit ordinary Cubans substantially more than the proceeds of state-owned facilities.

Thus, to speed the dynamic currently underway, we propose strengthening some of our previous recommendations.

1. *Issue a General License for Travel by All Americans.* Following the Clinton administration's January 1999 measures, new travel regulations have effectively expanded licensing for American travel to Cuba—to nearly 200,000 for 1999, by most estimates. Trusting in the power of freedom and democracy, and in view of the success of people-to-people contacts, we recommend that the president issue a general license to all Americans wishing to travel to Cuba. Americans traveling freely, without government licensing or program restrictions, will support the expansion of free-market activity in Cuba and will build links with Cuban society that no government program would envision. If the Cuban government blocks Americans from visiting the island, it alone will be held responsible for isolating the Cuban population. American citizens personify American

ideas and values. We note that despite the recent codification of travel regulations, the House of Representatives voted recently to lift the travel ban indirectly by withholding the funds needed to enforce current restrictions. Whether through a change in law by Congress, which would be preferable, or through the existing licensing authority of the executive branch, all Americans should now be able to travel freely to Cuba. The effect of a general license for all American travel will be to eliminate the current requirement of prior approval from OFAC; it will thereby end the ban on travel to Cuba by Americans excluded by current regulations.

2. *Make Federal Funds Available to Support People-to-People Exchanges.* According to OFAC, more than 200 American NGOs are currently engaged in some sort of exchange with Cuban institutions. At present, only a handful of private foundations support these exchanges. Many of the American NGOs now building new ties with Cuban institutions receive federal funds for a range of their international activities, including from the National Endowment for the Arts, the National Endowment for the Humanities, the National Science Foundation, the National Endowment for Democracy, the Fulbright Scholarship Program, the United States Information Agency (USIA), as well as from the Inter-American Foundation and many sources at other executive branch agencies, such as the Department of Education, the Department of Agriculture, the Environmental Protection Agency, as well as the Smithsonian Institution. But current practices reduce the potential impact of these programs by preventing NGOs from spending these funds for licensed exchanges and forcing them to compete instead for limited funds from private foundations. We therefore recommend an end to the current practice of prohibiting the use of such funds to support American NGOs' people-to-people programs with Cuba, which include programs between American and Cuban official and independent trade unions, and sponsorship for undergraduate, postgraduate, and mid-career study by Cubans in the United States and Americans in Cuba. In

addition, Cuban professionals should be invited for USIA-sponsored international education tours. We also recommend an increase in the number of staff at the U.S. Interests Section to help facilitate the emergent partnerships between American and Cuban NGOs and private foundations. And finally, we urge private sector and U.S. government support for book and literature programs focused on democracy and market reform. Such materials should be made available to Cuban religious organizations, students, scholars, and independent civic groups.

3. *Direct Commercial Flights and Ferry Service.* In our last report, we recommended that the United States permit commercial airlines to open routes from major U.S. cities and hubs to Havana and other Cuban cities. Since then, charter service has expanded from Miami, New York, and Los Angeles to Havana, Santiago, Camagüey, and other cities. We again recommend that commercial airlines be permitted to fly to Cuba. To that end, we recommend that the United States negotiate a civil aviation agreement with Cuba. In addition, we recommend that OFAC be authorized to issue licenses for regular ferry services between Florida and Havana.

4. *Expand Links Between American NGOs and their Cuban Counterparts to Promote Environmental Health and Conservation.* Americans and Cubans have a common interest in protecting species such as manatees, sea turtles, and migratory birds that share an ecosystem. The long-term health of the Cuban population and its prospects for future prosperity will depend on the wise stewardship of the Cuban environment. Conservationists within Cuba can provide an important counterpoint to those who would despoil critical ecosystems such as the Biramas and Zapata wetlands, or the remaining forests of the Sierra Maestra and Sierra del Rosario. Yet restrictions on developing joint programs with their Cuban counterparts hamper American NGOs' efforts to build exchanges in the area of environmental conservation. For example, joint environmental research between American NGOs and scientists at Cuban universities and research institutes is hindered by restrictions

that prohibit the transfer of funds and equipment for joint field-based activities. This is because research scientists tend to be based at universities, research institutions such as botanical gardens, and centers such as the Institute of Ecology. Although these entities can be defined as branches of the Cuban government, the technical specialists working there are individuals who will be active in conserving Cuba's environment well into the future, beyond the current regime. An investment in developing cooperative environmental and wildlife-conservation projects between the United States and Cuba would receive broad support in both countries. We therefore recommend issuing the requisite licensing to American NGOs for the purpose of transferring funds and equipment for joint field-based activities.

BASKET THREE: SECURITY

Whatever the precise shape Cuba's future political evolution takes, the Cuban military will likely play an important role, either permitting or seeking to suppress a peaceful democratic transition.

Among the most heartening trends in eastern Europe—with the exception of Yugoslavia—have been the strongly positive roles that the military forces in a number of the former Soviet satellites have played. Many NATO generals served as officers in the armed forces of former communist regimes. This is true even in Poland, where as recently as 1986, the Polish Army was enforcing martial law against the Solidarity trade union. In our own hemisphere—in El Salvador, for example—former guerrillas now participate in the democratic process and have become political party activists and elected officials. We note also that the Southern Command (SouthCom) has begun to interact with the Nicaraguan army, once under total control of the Frente Sandinista de Liberación Nacional (FSLN), but now serving under elected civilian rule.

We hope the Cuban armed forces will move down the same road and accept civilian control in a future democratic state. We believe that as the Cuban armed forces gain confidence that the United States will not take military advantage of a political opening on the island (as government propaganda claims), the more likely it is that the armed forces will permit, or even support, such an opening in the future. We want to enhance the chances that this will happen.

Some Task Force members are reluctant to grant the present Cuban regime and its military and security agencies the legitimacy that the exchange recommendations listed below seem to imply. These members emphasize, in any event, that such exchanges can serve U.S. interests only if they involve mid-level, younger officers in the Cuban armed forces, not merely the most senior—and presumably most ideologically committed—officers. These Task Force members emphasize also the value of civilian-to-military exchanges: they note that the United States should encourage the armed forces in former communist nations that have carried out successful transitions to democracy, such as Poland, to conduct similar exchanges with the Cuban armed forces. Finally, they stress that one of the central messages that the U.S. military should convey to its Cuban counterparts is that future relations, and indeed the status of the Cuban military itself, will depend significantly on whether it plays a constructive role in a peaceful, democratic transition.

We share these concerns and believe that any program of military-to-military contact should be designed accordingly, and that such contacts be carefully calibrated and reviewed regularly. Nevertheless, although we recognize the risks involved, we take a pragmatic, realistic view. The Cuban military exists. Indeed, it is one of the few strong institutions on the island. Its attitudes and behavior will be crucial to Cuba's future political course. We believe that the vital interests of the United States will be served by taking steps now to prepare for that future.

1. *Develop Military-to-Military Contacts.* Several former Commanders-in-Chief (CINCs) with responsibility for the

Caribbean, such as General Jack Sheehan and General Charles Wilhem, have stated that the Commander-in-Chief, Southern Command (CINCSOUTHCOM), and his staff should be able to sit down with their Cuban counterparts to discuss security issues relevant to their responsibilities, in such areas as drugs, crime, joint disaster relief, and joint air-sea rescue. At a lower level, it would also be beneficial to promote contacts at the 0–4 and 0–5 rank (lieutenant commanders and commanders, majors, and lieutenant colonels). On the Cuban side, these officers will be in key positions of responsibility seven to ten years from now, so now is the best time to start developing the kinds of professional ties and relationships that will facilitate future communication, dialogue, cooperation, and better mutual understanding. If, after a trial period, the United States determines that such engagement is having no constructive effect or that the Cuban government is manipulating and limiting the contacts so as to nullify their purpose, the nature and scale of the engagement can be reviewed.

2. *Continue Counternarcotic Contacts.* It is in the interests of the United States to develop an active program of counternarcotic contacts with Cuban counterparts, through the exchange of information regarding drug trafficking and organized crime. Cuba is geographically central to the drug economy of the Caribbean Basin. Regarding drug trafficking, the program goals would be to cooperate in the exchange of information related to the shipment of drugs through, over, and around Cuba and the Caribbean, whether the drugs' ultimate destination is Cuba or the United States. The intelligence to be shared would be the information useful for deterring and suppressing the drug trade. Intelligence exchanges focused on information related to the drug trade and organized crime would be beneficial to the United States and support the broader U.S. objective of a more stable, peaceful, and prosperous Caribbean Basin. At a minimum, this interaction should involve some limited exchanges of personnel between both countries to foster cooperation on these vital matters of mutual interest. If Cuba's

public commitment to battle the drug menace in the Caribbean proves hollow, and the counternarcotic-exchange effort yields no early harvest, the endeavor should be discontinued.

3. *Explore Regional Cooperation on Colombia.* We note that Colombia has invited Cuba to join with Norway, France, Spain, and Switzerland in a group of *países amigos* (friendly countries) to "accompany" Colombia in its search for a negotiated settlement to the country's conflicts. The government of Colombia has indicated that, particularly with respect to the Ejercito de Liberación Nacional (ELN) guerrillas, the government of Cuba has played a constructive role in the negotiations. We recommend that the United States government actively and formally work with Cuba, if the opportunity presents itself, in support of the Colombian peace process.

BASKET FOUR: TRADE, INVESTMENT, PROPERTY,
AND LABOR RIGHTS

Our last report recommended a series of measures designed to relieve the suffering of the Cuban people today while building the basis for a better relationship between Cuba and the United States in the future. Here, we elaborate on some of these proposals and include additional recommendations that focus on two fundamentals that Cuba will need to address in the future: labor rights and the legacy of property nationalizations.

1. *Food and Medicine Exports.* In January 1999, the White House—echoing this Task Force's earlier recommendation—announced that it would open up commercial sales of food and medicine to Cuba. However, when the new regulations were promulgated five months later, they banned private financing and limited food sales to "independent, nongovernmental entities," noting that "end users" must have no relationship with the Cuban government.

Prior to the final congressional vote on sanctions reform in October 2000, bipartisan majorities in the House and Senate voted to end the sanctions on sales of food and medicine to Cuba without the private-financing restrictions carried under the new law. Recognizing the bipartisan support that now exists, this Task Force recommends that whether by law or by presidential policy, all sales of food, agricultural products and inputs, and medicine and medical products to nongovernmental institutions, governmental agencies, and private citizens in Cuba be permitted, for cash or with conventional 90-day commercial (but not government-subsidized) credits. Currently, the Cuban government does not permit private farmers and independent small businesses to cooperate in purchasing U.S. food or medical products or inputs. We call upon the government of Cuba to permit all "end users" to purchase these American products.

2. *Permit Investment in and Export of Newly Created Informational Products.* The 1988 Omnibus Trade Bill amended the Trading with the Enemy Act to legalize the export of informational material to countries otherwise subject to the act's prohibitions. The Treasury Department interpreted the new law to include exports of only finished products such as published books, compact discs, artwork, movies, and so on. The original intent of the new law was to allow Americans to export not only these finished products, but also to invest in the production for export of newly created informational materials. Consistent with Recommendation Four in this basket, we recommend, as we did in our first report, that OFAC be instructed to revise existing regulations to permit direct American investment in the creation and export of new informational products.

3. *Facilitate Resolution of Expropriation Claims.* President Eisenhower banned U.S. trade with Cuba forty years ago, in October of 1960, in response to Cuba's nationalization-without-compensation of properties and businesses then owned by Americans on the island. Cuba had taken over agricultural lands

and sugar mills soon after the 1959 revolution; in 1960 it seized the U.S.-controlled nickel mines, the telephone company, petroleum refineries, electrical generation and distribution facilities, cement and tire plants, supermarkets, and banks.

Excluding individual (largely residential property) claims, the U.S. Foreign Claims Settlement Commission (FCSC) valued the U.S. corporate properties taken at $1.6 billion in 1972. Calculating interest at the rate of 6 percent utilized by the FCSC, this gross loss would be roughly $5.52 billion today, though the impact on the companies has been reduced by tax benefits.

The embargo was tightened by President John F. Kennedy in February of 1962. It has remained in place ever since. Titles III and IV of the 1996 Helms-Burton law—the provisions that penalize foreign companies and have created serious tensions with Europe and Canada—are both directed at foreigners who "traffic" in the expropriated U.S. property.

The uncompensated claims of U.S. citizens, in short, have been central to the U.S.-Cuba confrontation for four decades. As a first step toward resolving the claims issue, we propose a solution that would be more meaningful to the business prospects of the expropriated U.S. companies than would be the uncertain possibility of some discounted cash recovery at some future date from a future Cuban government for their net losses, after taxes, for property taken more than forty years ago. The proposal would at the same time reduce the likelihood of confrontation between the United States and its allies over Helms-Burton.

Our recommendation requires some background. In recent years, the Cuban government has legalized dollar holdings and transactions, delegated authority to managers of the state enterprises, and enacted Law Number 77, entitled the Foreign Investment Act (Law 77), which establishes a framework for foreign investment in joint ventures in Cuba.

A number of European and Canadian companies have entered into joint ventures with Cuban state companies. Others are under active consideration. In at least one case involving property confiscated from U.S. claimant ITT, the

Italian phone company STET reached a settlement with ITT as a result of which STET was able to enter into a joint venture with the Cuban telephone company without facing a risk of challenge under Helms-Burton.

Like the Europeans and Canadians, certain U.S. companies with claims certified by the FCSC are interested in future business opportunities in Cuba. Many of these "certified claimants" are prepared to resolve their forty-year-old nationalization claims against the Cuban government in the context of joint-venture agreements with the relevant Cuban enterprises, through which they would again be able to participate in—and contribute to—the Cuban economy. They would do so by renouncing their certified claims in exchange for equity in joint-venture projects under Law 77.

Such resolution of a certified claim is not inconsistent with Helms-Burton. It is the essence of the statute that a determination not to pursue a claim, or its abandonment or relinquishment, requires no authorization from the U.S. government. The decision is the certified claimant's to make. Title III establishes that claimants—both certified and noncertified—have causes of action against "traffickers" (which, for the moment, they cannot pursue because of the suspension of Title III access to U.S. federal courts). But Title III does not require a claimant to sue to obtain a recovery. A claimant may litigate or desist as the claimant chooses. Settlement of a claim in the context of a joint venture would be, in substance, nothing more than a voluntary decision to desist from pursuing a Title III suit.

The transaction by which the U.S. company may propose to enter into a joint venture with the Cuban enterprise would have to be licensed under the present regulatory scheme—and it could be licensed. Helms-Burton "codified" the embargo of Cuba as it stood on March 1, 1996. It thus preserved the ban on U.S. persons engaging in business transactions in Cuba in the absence of a license, "except as specifically authorized by the U.S. Secretary of Treasury."[8] Thus, the proposed settlements

---

[8]Section 515.201(b)(1) of the Cuban Assets Control Regulations.

could be licensed under the economic embargo of Cuba in effect on March 1, 1996, consistent with Helms-Burton.

We recognize that this proposal addresses only claims certified by the FCSC and not claims by Cuban Americans who lost property. Some members of our Task Force believe the American government should espouse the property claims of Cuban Americans. Others believe doing so would reinforce the current Cuban government's nationalist rhetoric and also be highly destabilizing to a new, democratic government. They argue that this issue should instead be left to another day, and properly subject to judicial proceedings in a future democratic Cuba.

We limit our present recommendations to a first step toward addressing what will inevitably prove a long and complicated process involving the claims of American citizens, whatever future political course Cuba takes. We believe, however, that the opportunity to resolve the vexing expropriation claims should not be limited to the claims of business enterprises. Any holder or transferee of a claim should be permitted to negotiate an exchange of that claim for whatever value is deemed adequate to satisfy that claim. In short, other exchanges of value, in addition to participation in a joint venture, should be permitted (and indeed encouraged); the sooner this bone of contention can be resolved and the ancient claims disposed of the better.

At this time we recommend that the president prepare to issue licenses for the purpose of negotiating and implementing such settlements as we describe herein.

The proposal—to allow expropriation claims against Cuba to be resolved by claimants as part of a joint-venture arrangement—raises the issue of whether U.S claimants who settle existing claims in exchange for equity positions in their original, or other, industries, would then be free to invest and expand on their equity, or would remain passive owners only. Without the ability to further capitalize their investment, some claimants might have less incentive to go forward. On the other hand, to allow them to invest without limitation might be seen as creating a privileged class of individuals and companies—either the original claimants or those who had purchased rights to a claim—who would be legally allowed to invest in Cuba, to the exclusion and perhaps commercial disadvantage of all other U.S. individuals and companies. The Task Force chose not to resolve this point. There seemed to be a consensus for taking the first step of allowing U.S. claims to be resolved through equity ownership, but not a consensus in favor of the next step of allowing follow-on investments by the new U.S equity owners. Some suggested that the discriminatory effect was reason to reject the proposal; others thought that the logical solution was to license investment generally.

The dilemma, in other words, raised a broader issue that reached beyond the mandate the Task Force had set for itself: whether removing the present ban on U.S. investment in Cuba is in the national interest and would promote a rapid, peaceful transition to democracy in Cuba. The debate has often been articulated elsewhere in narrow and sterile terms—whether the United States should simply lift the embargo or tighten it, as a means to alter the political structure in Cuba. Not enough thought has been given to the possibility of allowing U.S. investment in Cuba subject to certain norms that would promote human and worker rights and the evolution of independent trade unions. Around the world, U.S. corporations are taking the lead in adopting codes of conduct that make many important standards—regarding child labor, working hours and conditions, human rights, sexual harassment, and nondiscrimination—a condition of partnership with producers.

We think a serious discussion among those who wish to see a more thoughtful and creative policy toward Cuba needs to begin about this subject. Certainly, U.S. policy toward communist countries such as China and Vietnam has evolved toward engagement by the U.S. private sector, as an instrument of opening markets and stimulating democratic change. In South Africa, such codes of conduct promoted by American companies played a constructive role in that society's evolution from authoritarian racism to multiracial democracy. As with the Task

Force's debate on claims settlement, the subject of U.S. investment in Cuba needs the same kind of creative and pragmatic thinking.

Opponents of lifting the ban on investment argue that, given the economic structure of joint ventures in Cuba, investment would simply channel hard-currency reserves into the regime, strengthen its capacity for political control and repression, and thus perpetuate the regime. This is a serious concern. However, the Task Force, in both its first and second reports, also reached a consensus that engagement with Cuba, through significantly expanded people-to-people exchanges, on balance promotes democratic change. The fact is that such exchanges—by bringing hundreds of thousands of Americans to Cuba—also bring additional hard currency to the government. So too do others of our recommendations: lifting the current limit on remittances by Cuban Americans; extending remittances to all Americans; ending the limit on visits by Cuban Americans to their families; lifting the ban on travel by all Americans; and permitting limited investment on the island to support these activities and its small but growing private sector. Therefore, much more open and creative thought must be given to judging the real effects of U.S. investment. Practices around the world suggest that, in general, U.S. corporations overall are far more likely to impose codes of conduct, direct payment of workers, and other labor and human rights as a condition of investment. Moreover, substantial evidence exists to show that workers in firms in which non-U.S. investors are involved also reap substantial economic benefits—despite the clear effort by the Cuban government to control hiring and siphon off a substantial percentage of workers' earnings. These benefits allow them to provide better for their families and also reduce their economic dependence on the government, which remains an important lever of its social control. Although the Task Force has chosen not to join the investment debate outright, we believe strongly that there is a need to try to find creative new ideas that could break the old deadlock on issues of investment, such as outlined above, and promote the goal that unites Americans of good faith: promoting rapid, peaceful, democratic change in Cuba.

4. *Begin Licensing Some American Business Activity.* The Cuban government has been slow to enact liberalizing economic reforms. It prohibits, for example, Cuban citizens from investing in small businesses on the island. We believe that permitting certain limited American investment on the island can further the economic reform process in Cuba and begin to help all Cubans to participate fully in their economy. To that end, we reiterate a recommendation from our first report: that four limited categories of American business routinely receive licenses to operate in Cuba. As in our first report, these categories of business activity are: 1) news gathering or the procurement and creation of informational material; 2) providing on-the-ground services to capture the business resulting from increased American and Cuban-American travel; 3) activities related to the distribution of humanitarian aid and sales; and 4) activities related to culture, including the production, purchase, and sale of new cultural materials and artworks, such as theater, music, architectural preservation and restoration, photography, urban planning, and the media, and the verification of Cuban adherence to intellectual property rights. In our judgment, each of these categories supports objectives clearly specified in U.S. law.

In addition, one of the greatest obstacles to the development of an independent trade union movement in Cuba and to greater rates of foreign investment is the monopoly the state currently holds on the hiring and paying of workers. As it becomes apparent that Cuba is reducing the role of the state in the hiring process, we recommend consideration of American investment beyond these four categories, contingent upon demonstrated progress in adhering to workers' core labor rights, as identified by the International Labor Organization (ILO).[9]

---

[9]The ILO adopts international labor standards in the form of Conventions and Recommendations setting minimum standards on fundamental labor rights: freedom of association and the right to collective bargaining, elimination of all forms of forced and compulsory labor, effective abolition of child labor, elimination of discrimination in respect of employment and occupation, and other standards regulating conditions across the entire spectrum of work-related issues. Source: *ILO: What it Does* (Geneva, Switzerland: International Labor Organization, 2000), p. 2.

5. *Conduct an Independent Study of Labor Rights in Cuba.* The development of a free and independent trade union movement, and protection of core labor rights such as the right to strike and organize, count among the foundations of democracy. We note the leading role played by the independent Solidarity trade union movement in Poland, with strong support from the AFL-CIO, and by trade unions in South Africa in the successful transition to democracy and the end of apartheid, respectively. Today, many core ILO standards and internationally recognized labor rights are denied in Cuba, where official trade unions largely serve the interests of the state. The current Cuban law, to cite just one example, that requires foreign investors to contract workers indirectly, violates internationally recognized labor rights. The overall result is that foreign investors pay several hundred dollars per month per worker, but the worker receives a fraction of that amount in pesos. This amounts to a labor tax of approximately 90 percent. This tax, along with many other economic hardships and inequities experienced by Cuban workers, grows out of their fundamental inability to exercise the right to free association and collective bargaining. Foreign investors as a rule supplement this base pay with monthly dollar bonuses and basic hygiene and food products. Indeed, even many state enterprises and some government institutions now supplement peso salaries with regular dollar bonuses. Earlier in the 1990s, coveted jobs in the mixed-enterprise sectors were once reserved for party loyalists and the military. Today, jobs in tourism and related services, private and cooperative farming, and microenterprises have expanded. It has thus become much more difficult for the government to subject hiring practices to a political litmus test.

Cuban workers can and should play an important and positive role in a peaceful democratic transition to a society capable of protecting existing social benefits for workers, while also sharing the benefits of the new global economy with all of its working people. As we have seen from the experiences in the former Soviet Union and many nations of eastern Europe, this is a daunting but essential task. The AFL-CIO and the International Confederation of Free Trade Unions (ICFTU) have recently led delegations to Cuba to discuss the fundamental importance of an independent trade-union movement in the defense of workers' rights, and how best to prepare the Cuban labor force to function in a more open economy. The process of dialogue and discussion needs to be broadened and deepened. We therefore recommend an independently funded study of labor rights in the mixed- and state-enterprise sectors, comparing Cuban law and conditions to those of comparable economies in the region and to basic worker rights guaranteed under the ILO. The study should also examine the issue of race and ethnicity in the Cuban work force to examine the extent to which Cubans of color have equal access to jobs in the joint-venture sectors, especially tourism. Such a study should draw on the work in this area already done by the AFL-CIO and by other research conducted on the ground in Cuba, to provide interested parties—such as American and international trade unions, businesses, and human rights groups—with a baseline of information, and to suggest directions for further initiatives to prepare Cuban workers and management for their inevitable encounter with the demands of the global economy. We recommend that after the study is completed, the U.S. administration consult with labor, business, and congressional leaders to discuss how to implement its findings.

6. *License American Universities and the Private Sector to Establish Management Training and Labor Rights Institutes.* In recent years, Cuba has been sending young managers of joint-venture enterprises to Europe for training in business management. Among the most competitive fields in Cuba, now attracting some of the brightest young people, are international law, business, and economics. Indeed, the mixed-enterprise sector continues to expand, providing a training ground for those individuals who will emerge as the forces driving the emergence of a market economy. The American private sector, directly and through university programs, can play a valuable role in this process. We recommend that the president issue

licenses to American businesses, business schools, and NGOs to establish management training institutes in Cuba with European, Canadian, and Latin American partners. We likewise recommend that Cuban students be awarded scholarships, to be paid by universities and the private sector, to attend business school and management training programs in the United States. We believe a similar program should be considered in cooperation with the AFL-CIO, to educate Cuban workers about internationally recognized labor rights and the organizing of free trade unions. Finally, we call on the government of Cuba to permit its students and other citizens to take advantage of such opportunities as they arise.

7. *Support Cuban Observer Status in the International Monetary Fund, the World Bank, and Inter-American Development Bank.* Since the collapse of the Soviet bloc, the Cuban government has undertaken sporadic economic reforms, but has rejected a comprehensive liberalization of the economy. We recognize that Cuba has a considerable distance to go and much to learn about how modern market economies and the international financial system function before it will be eligible for full membership in the international financial institutions. The process of exposing Cuba to the norms and practices of the international community should include giving Cubans the opportunity to understand those institutions that are relevant to implementing economic reforms, which will be necessary to compete in the global economy. As a first step in laying the groundwork for an economic transition in Cuba, we recommend that the International Monetary Fund, the World Bank, and the Inter-American Development Bank consider granting Cuba observer status.

8. *Oppose Cuba's Readmission to the Organization of American States (OAS).* Admission to the OAS is another matter. The OAS and its member states labored long and hard over the last decade to strengthen the institution's commitment to

democracy as the only legitimate form of government in the Western Hemisphere and to take on a collective responsibility, as first enunciated in the Santiago Declaration in June 1991, to defend democracy when it is at risk. We believe Cuba's readmission to the OAS now would undermine that important institutional commitment to democracy. Therefore, until Cuba accepts the democratic disciplines of regular, free elections embraced by every other nation in the region, we oppose its readmission to the OAS.

ADDITIONAL AND DISSENTING
VIEWS BY MEMBERS

On Addressing Lifting the U.S. Embargo

We strongly support the Task Force's recommendations but believe that its objectives can be best achieved by addressing the central issue of U.S.-Cuban relations: the embargo.

The current U.S. embargo obstructs humanitarian aid and obscures the failure of the Cuban government's economic policies, which is the central cause of the very significant human suffering in Cuba today. The new president has an historic opportunity to work with a new Congress to lift the embargo, specifically all restrictions on trade and travel, and he should be encouraged to do so.

We agree with the report's conclusion, however, that the ban on American investment should be treated differently. It should only be lifted as the Cuban government allows Cuban citizens to participate in the Cuban economy through direct employment, business ownership, and other economic rights.

María de Lourdes Duke
Micho Fernandez Spring

On Travel and People-to-People Exchanges

There are two reasons why, in spite of some differences in tone and even in content, I am willing to sign this report. One is that it properly assumes that the task before us is to devise a policy for the middle and longer term, taking as a given the biological fact of Fidel Castro's mortality. The other is that the report largely frees us from the trap of waiting for reciprocity from Havana. That will never come under the present regime. A proper U.S.

policy toward Cuba takes its point of departure from the notion that we know what we want. Whether the current government of Cuba—which after all has never been elected—wants it too should properly be a matter of indifference to us. As we are not omnipotent, or even "hegemonic," we may not get where we want to go, but that should not stop us from identifying and using the many assets we do possess.

Cuba is a very special Latin American country. Although supposedly very nationalistic, it is nonetheless permanently fascinated by and attracted to the United States—our culture, our institutions, our way of life. Indeed, I would not be a bit surprised to see the next government in Cuba, or the ones that follow it, among the most pro–United States in the island's history. The parts of the report with which I am most in sympathy are the ones that seek to build upon the preternatural disposition toward friendliness and admiration that exists among broad sectors of the Cuban people (and, for all we can know, may even seep up into the lower rungs of the political and military leadership).

I likewise believe that any effort to increase the contact between Cubans on the island and their relatives in the United States is bound to serve our common long-term purposes, by providing the Cuban people with a more complete and accurate view of the world outside, puncturing the walls of propaganda and disinformation behind which the Cuban people are forced to dwell.

For the same reason I now find myself favorably disposed to the notion of lifting the ban on tourist travel. Quite apart from the fact that the ban itself is becoming increasingly difficult to enforce (thousands of Americans visit the island each year illegally by traveling through third countries), for many years to come Cuba will be in no position to provide hostelling for the number of Americans that will want to visit. This means that our people will have to stay in Cuban homes. This will provide a source of independent hard-currency income for many families, with the potential to create alternative poles of economic power in a society where the government uses scarcity as a primary tool of domination.

Mark Falcoff

Although this report recommends an end to the ban on travel by all Americans to Cuba and increased exchanges across fields, as a matter of emphasis, I believe it is important to stress expanded cultural activities and exchanges. This includes exhibitions, historic preservation, literature and poetry, theater, media arts, photography, dance, opera, musical presentations—both classical and modern—architectural design, and the graphic arts, as well as facilitating the expansion of people-to-people programs that include travel from and to Cuba by artists and students as well as presenting exhibitions and performances. Moreover, I wish to emphasize that outside of the realm of business, on the one hand, or federal funding, on the other, there is a vast realm of society itself that should be engaged in supporting exchanges and contacts of this nature.

Wendy W. Luers

People-to-people contacts are desirable only if they help level the playing field between the Cuban people and the Cuban government. Allowing unrestricted travel to Cuba by U.S. citizens under existing conditions in Cuba would overwhelmingly benefit the Cuban government at the expense of the Cuban people. The government owns all hotels. Cubans who work in the tourism sector cannot be paid directly or in hard currency. Instead, their wages are paid to the Cuban government, which then exchanges the hard currency into Cuban pesos at the artificial exchange rate of one peso for one dollar. Since the real exchange rate is about 20 pesos to the dollar, the Cuban government keeps approximately 95 cents of every dollar spent on hotels, food, and entertainment. Finally, people-to-people contact is limited by the fact that the Cuban government practices "tourism apartheid." Cubans cannot frequent the hotels or use the beaches on which they are located—a policy aimed at keeping foreigners segregated from the vast majority of Cubans on the island. If and when the Cuban government rescinds the above-mentioned practices, I would favor allowing any U.S. citizen wishing to visit Cuba to do so.

Susan Kaufman Purcell

On Federal Funding for NGOs

There should be no federal funding of NGOs operating in Cuba. Such funding automatically compromises the independence of the recipients. The Castro regime will seek every opportunity to portray ostensibly private organizations as nothing more than tools of the U.S. government, and this provision makes it more likely that such a campaign of vilification will be believed by the Cuban people.

Ted Galen Carpenter

On Independent Trade Unions and Labor Rights

While I share some of the concerns expressed by colleagues on the Task Force regarding relationships with Cuban authorities, I believe the report has succeeded in its objective of making recommendations that do not require any fundamental change in the status of the embargo. In concurring with the general policy thrust of the report, however, I would also make some additional comments consistent with the AFL-CIO Resolution of October 8, 1999, on Food and Medicine to Cuba, which has been distributed to members of the Task Force.

In promoting conditions for a peaceful transition to democracy in Cuba, we must also have realistic expectations and measurements for progress toward the legal recognition of independent labor unions, the release of political prisoners, the legalization of opposition political parties, and the holding of free and fair elections, among other steps necessary to bring about such a transition. If these steps were not to materialize within a reasonable period of time, reasonable people might well conclude that the basic assumption of the Task Force's approach was wrong.

The study of labor rights is well conceived, but it would be significantly strengthened with an active role by the ILO and by a serious commitment to follow through on whatever recommendations it might produce, as is implied by the recommendation in the last sentence for the administration to discuss implementation measures.

In discussing labor rights elsewhere in the document, too much emphasis is placed on the efficacy of corporate codes of conduct in protecting the rights of workers, particularly freedom of association and collective bargaining. The world has a universal standard on labor rights and their implementation. They are ILO Conventions and core labor standards. They need to be enforced, in Cuba and everywhere else in the world.

Jay Mazur

I support the insistence on labor rights. This is one of the few instances where the report actually demands something from the regime.

Peter W. Rodman

On Observer Status at the World Bank and Inter-American Development Bank

We support the recommendation that Cuba be given observer status at the World Bank and the Inter-American Development Bank so long as this status is offered with the agreement by the governing bodies of both institutions that Cuba would not be granted full membership until it conducts free and fair democratic multiparty elections.

Adrian Karatnycky
Susan Kaufman Purcell
Micho Fernandez Spring

One of the principal objectives of the report is to do nothing that would have "the primary effect of consolidating or legitimizing the status quo on the island." But in fact membership in such organizations is avidly sought by the present government to satisfy just that purpose. The Lomé organization, mentioned in the text, is a case in point. If economic education is what we seek, let Cuba—which already has an Interests Section in Washington—send some of its diplomats across town to "observe."

Mark Falcoff

The Task Force is correct to note that the Castro government has permitted some economic reforms—reforms forced by the loss of Soviet subsidies, not because of a fundamental change in Mr. Castro's philosophy. The problem on the island is the denial of freedom to the Cuban people, not a failure to "expos[e] Cuba to the norms and practices" of international financial institutions. The Cuban diaspora has shown its ability to prosper when it has been allowed to operate in a free society. The difference between Cubans on the island and those in exile is in the conditions under which the two parts of the Cuban community are able to conduct economic activities. Further, it is the Castro regime that would be given "observer status," not a freely chosen Cuban government. International Monetary Fund, World Bank, and Inter-American Development Bank observer status (and ultimately membership) should be predicated on a democratic Cuba.

Daniel W. Fisk

On Developing Further Military-to-Military Contacts

Part of the constructive contribution to the Cuba debate made by the Task Force is its effort to look beyond the Castro regime and propose policy changes that do not "have the primary effect of consolidating, or appearing to legitimize, the political status quo on the island." The recommendation to develop military-to-military contacts does not contribute to this objective. Mr. Castro's rule is based on the concept of a mobilized society and a strong centralized state directed by a vanguard party. The Cuban military (FAR) is a fundamental component of this vanguard. Control over the military is maintained by individual loyalty to Mr. Castro, the continuation of the party organization

and focus on political education within the military, and the professionalization of the FAR. Arguably, the professionalization of
the military is a double-edged sword for the regime, contribut-
ing to regime loyalty but also creating an atmosphere in which
a separate identity can be developed while gestures of loyalty are
mimicked. As one authority on the Cuban military noted, "the
regime's dilemma is in discerning among the true believers, the
sycophants, and the survivors." That, however, is also the dilemma confronting any U.S. engagement with the FAR, which
remains an instrument of the Castro government, with loyalty
to the Castro brothers still the dominant criteria for leadership.
At most the United States should continue the routine military-
to-military contacts related to the U.S. presence on Guantánamo
and continue licensing meetings between Cuban military officials and civilian, non–U.S. government military experts and
former U.S. military officials. Further, the U.S. government
should make clear, using Radio and TV Martí, our willingness
to engage with the military of a democratic Cuba. It should not
expand—or endeavor to expand—military-to-military contacts
with an instrument of the current Cuban government. This only
serves to legitimize the regime.

Mark Falcoff
Daniel W. Fisk

We endorse the main thrust of the Task Force report and most
of its recommendations, particularly those that seek to reach ordinary Cubans and nongovernmental segments of Cuban society
in the private sector and in a nascent, repressed civil society. We
cannot, however, endorse those recommendations that focus on
upgrading contacts with institutions that are instruments of
state power, particularly the section that recommends military-
to-military contacts. While such contacts might be helpful if—
as is posited in the report—they reached younger officers, they
are more likely—in reality—to be the basis for travel and

exchanges between our military with segments of the Cuban intelligence community.

Adrian Karatnycky
Susan Kaufman Purcell
Micho Fernandez Spring

The report would expand contacts with regime officials, notably the military. But this is based on a misreading of the experience in Central Europe, where the agents of change were not officials but opponents of the regime—Protestant clergy in East Germany, Solidarity and the Church in Poland, dissident intellectuals in Czechoslovakia. Purging the Party hacks from their institutions (academia, judiciary, professions, the military) has been the key to their progress. Expanding exchange with the Cuban military is particularly inappropriate. It is impossible for us to pretend to be sending signals for change of the regime while consorting with the security organs that maintain it. Ostracism will have better pedagogical value than seminars at Harvard.

Daniel W. Fisk
Peter Rodman

On Continuing Counternarcotic Contacts

There should be no cooperation on counternarcotics efforts. It is bad enough to endorse any new initiatives in Washington's futile and increasingly disruptive "supply-side" war on drugs. Even supporters of the prohibitionist strategy, though, should oppose collaboration with Cuban authorities. Joint measures between U.S. and Cuban agencies help legitimize the role of the Cuban military and, even worse, the Castro regime's internal security apparatus. The report recommends not only exchanges of information but "exchanges of personnel" between the two countries. Such collaboration sends precisely the wrong message to the Cuban people who view, correctly, the military and the internal security agencies as Castro's instruments of repression. A cautious dialogue with the Cuban military may be appropriate, but the Task Force Report should oppose more tangible linkages with the military and should oppose even opening a dialogue with the internal security bureaucracy.

Ted Galen Carpenter

We are wholly unpersuaded that Cuba is honestly interested in stemming the flow of drug traffic to the United States. The evidence, indeed, of Cuban involvement in trans-shipment and money-laundering is so significant as to make this subject a non-starter.

Mark Falcoff
Daniel W. Fisk
Susan Kaufman Purcell

On Regional Cooperation on Colombia

Whatever the government of Colombia may publicly say about Cuba's apparent support of the peace process, it is doubtful to me that the current Cuban government favors any outcome there even vaguely similar to that which we and other democratic "friends of Colombia" would wish to see.

Mark Falcoff
Daniel W. Fisk

We see no utility in inviting the Cuban government to become involved in peace efforts in Colombia. If Cuba has leverage with the rebels, it derives from Cuba's support or encouragement of their activities. If this is the case, Cuba deserves no place at the negotiating table.

Mark Falcoff
Adrian Karatnycky
Susan Kaufman Purcell
Micho Fernandez Spring

Additional and Dissenting Views by Members

On Facilitating a Resolution of Property Claims

The Task Force Report outlines an imaginative approach for beginning to resolve the certified claims of U.S. corporations who lost assets long ago, when Cuba expropriated nearly all private property.

I believe the time is at hand to go further and establish an orderly process for resolving the claims of Cuban Americans who later became U.S. citizens and, in the process, were deprived of their property by the Castro regime. Under traditional legal doctrines, the United States would not espouse the claims of persons who were not citizens when their property was taken. Traditional legal doctrines should not apply to Cuban Americans. In recent years, the United States has extended its moral authority, and its legal system, to victims of World War II who were not citizens when they suffered and died. Cuban Americans deserve no less.

In my view, an orderly process should build on four principles. First, the United States should espouse money compensation for Cuban Americans, not the physical return of their real estate. Second, the amount of money compensation for each claimant should be adjudicated by a claims settlement commission, to minimize delay and legal fees. Third, the United States should insist on realistic funding mechanisms, as it normalizes relations with Cuba, so that the principal and interest on claims can be paid within ten years. Finally, this new process should supercede Title III of the Helms-Burton Act, once normal relations are established with a new Cuba.

Gary Hufbauer

I believe the time is not yet ripe for settling outstanding disputes, but if certified claimants want to waste their time and resources talking to the present government, we should place no obstacle in their way. In the unlikely eventuality that they manage to resolve their claims now, no harm done. As to encouraging new U.S. investment, the notion that Cuba might—under the present political system—reduce (to what extent?) the role of the state in the hiring process is completely unrealistic and politically naïve. It is a contingency not even worth considering.

Mark Falcoff

The Task Force is to be commended for its attempt to address the complicated issue of expropriated properties. The report is correct in noting that a resolution of property claims "is not inconsistent with Helms-Burton," noting the agreement reached on the ITT property claim with the Italian phone company STET. Helms-Burton, however, was not premised upon an American property claimant's direct partnership with a Cuban government entity. Hence the agreement between ITT and STET, not ITT and the Cuban government. More significantly, the recommendation raises a potentially troubling precedent: in effect, it rewards the government that expropriated the property, leaving the individual property claimant in a position to negotiate the best deal with little or no leverage. The difference between the Helms-Burton remedy and this recommendation is that, under Helms-Burton, two litigants would appear before an impartial court as equals; under the Task Force recommendation, the American claimants would be going to Cuba as supplicants to an entity that is not only partial, but is actually an agent of the entity that took the property in the first place. This recommendation, while a topic for further discussion, raises a number of questions relevant to broader U.S. interests regarding Cuba and the protection of international property rights. In the absence of resolving such broader questions, we are concerned that the recommendation comes closer to legitimizing extortion than ratifying the rights of property claimants.

Daniel W. Fisk
Susan Kaufman Purcell

The report proposes allowing the settlement of expropriation claims in exchange for equity interest in joint ventures. This is a clever way to open a loophole in the embargo if one is looking for clever ways to open loopholes in the embargo. I am not. Easing the embargo on investment was supposed to be outside the scope of this inquiry. More important, it is something to be held in reserve until the regime enters some kind of transitional phase and there is a positive trend to reinforce. In the meantime, it is only a unilateral erosion of the U.S. position.

Peter W. Rodman

On the General Limitations of the Report

The Task Force's new report is more the product of impatience than of analysis. Two years ago, it produced a first report that went further than I thought made sense. Since then, nothing significant has happened except that the Elián González case has led (perhaps misled) some to conclude that the domestic political clout of the anti-Castro Cuban Americans has been broken. Those who are eager to restore ties with Cuba undoubtedly sensed an opportunity.

But the Castro regime remains as it was two years ago—a petty fascist dictatorship. This is not a regime in its Gorbachev or Khatami phase but in its Stalinist period. Any idea that the measures in this report will foster political change are an illusion.

Be that as it may, I continue to support (as I did in the last report) humanitarian measures that may expand the freedom of action of Cubans on the island, including economically, and that expand the freedom of action of Cuban Americans to exert influence there. The Basket One measures look good. I am agnostic about Basket Two, though a bit skeptical that they will have the leavening effect that is hoped for.

Baskets Three and Four are, for the most part, misconceived. The Task Force has pledged to avoid proposals that would challenge the embargo or legitimize the Castro regime. It has not been faithful to that pledge.

Peter W. Rodman

I refrain from endorsing this report due to my doubts that the statement of principle guiding the Task Force was satisfactorily honored. First, I believe that certain key recommendations that would significantly alter U.S. policy toward Cuba were not reasonably proven as leading to "rapid, peaceful, democratic change in Cuba while safeguarding the vital interests of the United States." In fact, if some of these policies were implemented, the economic and political control of the current totalitarian government of Cuba might be significantly enhanced, therefore actually hindering the Cuban people's ability to attain a favorable and rapid solution to their present predicament.

Second, I have an overall dissatisfaction with the methodology that guided the decision-making process within the Task Force's working sessions. As a result, key recommendations were ultimately included in the report despite the absence of an in-depth discussion based on factual information. Some were discussed in a hurry, most were approached with no background data or supporting materials to benefit Task Force members, especially those who lack expertise in certain areas within the scope of the report.

Third, I am disappointed by a lack of focus on objectively accounting for the actual effects of recent U.S. policy changes, especially those linked to the Task Force's prior recommendations. As a result, I did not find evidence that events in Cuba since the publishing of the first report have demonstrated that certain unconditional, unilateral policy actions on the part of the United States have advanced democratic change and, thus, merit further unilateral concessions in these areas.

Finally, I find Basket Three, "Security," particularly troubling for its seeming implication that Cuba no longer poses a threat to the security of the United States and, thus, merits increasing and friendly cooperation by our country. A more informed and balanced analysis of the nonconventional threats Cuba poses or may pose in the post–Cold War era was sorely lacking. Important issues such as Cuba's biochemical warfare capability, its continued harboring of international terrorists and fugitives from U.S. justice, and its ongoing participation in hemispheric subversion and drug trafficking were not addressed. The recommendations on security, thus, seem naïve, if not altogether deficient and misguided.

Notwithstanding the above, I support and endorse the stated intentions of this Task Force in an overall manner, as well as the dedication of each one of its members and facilitators to its explicit goals. Importantly, I believe in a policy of selective/conditional engagement to advance a timely transition to democracy in Cuba, and I trust that all who seek freedom for Cuba will continue to work in good faith to develop the right policies to help bring it about.

Maria C. Werlau

ADDITIONAL AND DISSENTING
VIEWS BY OBSERVERS*

On the Trade Sanctions Reform and Export Enhancement Act

I concur with the general policy thrust of the Task Force and believe the recommendations in this report will serve to advance U.S. policy to Cuba in a bipartisan fashion. The report makes an appropriate departure from the 1999 report in recognizing that members of Congress must play a significant role in the formulation of Cuba policy. The policy recommendations contained in the report provide a foundation for greater coordination with the executive branch in an area of elevated congressional interest.

While the report pointedly notes the shortcomings of legislation recently enacted to lift food and medicine sanctions on Cuba, it fails to acknowledge, on balance, the significance of this measure in advancing overall U.S.-Cuban relations.

The act prohibits the extension of U.S. government or commercial credit to Cuba for sales, while explicitly allowing third-country financing or sales with cash in advance. Criticism of this provision is misleading since in 1999, the Task Force recommended that the president "authoriz[e] all necessary financial transactions for cash payments on a noncredit basis." The act goes no further than this recommendation.

Any constraint of the president's ability to pursue greater people-to-people contacts will be relatively slight, as the codification of existing regulations protects travel-related transactions for all of the following activities: family visits, official business of the U.S. government, foreign governments and intergovern-

---

*All Task Force observers, other than those in the executive branch, were given the opportunity to submit written comments. The absence of such comments by some observers does not imply either their endorsement or dissent from the report of specific recommendations contained herein.

mental organizations, journalistic activity, professional research, educational activities, religious activities, public performances, clinics, workshops, athletic and other competitions and exhibitions, support for the Cuban people, humanitarian projects, and activities of private foundations or educational institutes. An additional category of travel is even created to allow commercial exports of agricultural commodities. The examples of potentially restricted activities cited in the report are truly at the fringe of desirable people-to-people activities. The legislative history further indicates that the authors of the act did not intend to derogate from current law or the flexibility provided for in existing regulations.

This act supersedes the requirements of the Cuban Liberty and Democratic Solidarity Act that would have required regime change before any modification to the embargo could be effected. As such, the enactment of this measure represents a significant, bipartisan shift toward limited engagement with Cuba and an opening that cannot be easily reversed. Food and medicine sanctions on Cuba may only be reimposed at the request of the president and by an affirmative vote of both the House and the Senate.

We do well to call for changes in U.S. policy, but we must also acknowledge that more dramatic change is unlikely unless the Cuban government demonstrates reciprocity. A new consensus is emerging, but will only be sustained if Cuba can demonstrate in good faith that it is willing to entertain additional contact with the United States.

Robert R. Neal

On the General Limitations of the Report

The goal of the original Task Force Report, the thrust of which I generally supported, was to lay aside the debate over the efficacy of the Cuban embargo, and work to find consensus on ways the United States could reach out to the Cuban people and support Cuban civil society in preparation for a post-Castro democratic transition.

Unfortunately, in its second report the Task Force has strayed from this guiding principle. It advocates lifting the embargo on tourism in Cuba, lifting all restrictions on food and medicine sales, and a proposal to resolve expropriation claims by giving U.S. businesses equity interest in foreign joint ventures (which, as Peter Rodman rightly points out, is a back-channel way to permit direct U.S. investment in Cuba). For these reasons, the new report is very disappointing.

The framework of U.S. Cuba policy should be to isolate the Castro regime, while working to end Castro's isolation of the Cuban people, by encouraging programs that foster and support an independent civil society—not engaging the Cuban government.

First, a point of clarification. I was astounded to read the following statement in the introduction of the report: "In March 2000, Senate Foreign Relations Committee Chairman Jesse Helms (R-N.C.) included in an authorizations bill an amendment ending sanctions on the sale of food and medicine to Cuba." As I made clear in a Task Force meeting, Senator Helms opposed the amendment in question. He let it through his committee only because the votes were not there to defeat it, but worked (successfully) with Republican leaders in the House and Senate to ensure it did not become law until further restrictions were added. Why the Task Force staff felt the need to give the false and misleading impression that Senator Helms supports ending all sanctions on the sale of food and medicine to Cuba is a mystery to me—and unnecessarily undermines the credibility of the entire report.

As the report notes, the compromise language that became law this year prevents any government credits or private financing of sales to Cuba, and codifies the U.S. travel ban on Cuba. Tightening the travel ban in exchange for a minimal easing of restrictions on food and medicine sales was, in the end, a good trade-off.

As a result of this codification of the travel embargo, the Task Force recommendation to lift the U.S. tourism travel ban is essentially moot. This is a good thing. Cuba practices tourism apartheid, and ordinary Cubans are not permitted anywhere near the exclusive hotels and resorts where Western tourists stay—unless they are employed there or are selling their bodies. Allowing U.S. tourists to flood Cuba's beaches and resorts would have done nothing more to encourage democratic change than tourists visiting South Africa's "Sun City" resort contributed to ending apartheid.

As for federal funding of NGOs for people-to-people exchanges, the U.S. government already spends $5 million a year to assist NGOs working to promote democracy in Cuba. This program, which is specifically targeted at supporting an *independent* civil society in Cuba and those working for democratic change, should be continued and expanded. But the U.S. government should by no means provide funding for programs with Cuban government institutions—such as exchanges with Cuba's official "trade unions" and the environmental groups the Task Force suggests—which would do nothing to help Cubans build an independent civil society. U.S. tax dollars should be used to support groups seeking to create space for Cubans outside the Cuban state—not to support programs *of* the Cuban state.

I agree with those who dissent from the recommendations for military-to-military contacts and counternarcotics contacts. These violate the Task Force's principle of not recommending any change in policy that has "the primary effect of consolidating, or appearing to legitimize," the Cuban regime. The United States certainly could and should develop innovative ways to reach out to the junior officers in the Cuban military, and make them aware of the experience of the militaries in Central European nations (who did not fire on the crowds when change came, and were as a result given a place of honor in the new democratic society). There are many ways this could be done: through NGOs, use of the international mail, and creative new programming on Radio Martí. Unfortunately, the Task Force has not recommended any such measures. Instead it has recommended cooperation with the Cuban military—measures that would be used by Castro to legitimize his regime.

The proposals on labor rights have merit, and are unique among the report's recommendations in that they actually require something of the Cuban regime. But the recommendations to give Cuba observer status at the World Bank and Inter-American Development Bank are misguided—like other recommendations for government-to-government collaboration—because they do not. All of these concessions to the government should be held back and used as leverage for the time when Castro is gone, and a transitional regime will be searching for ways to negotiate an end to Cuba's isolation in exchange for real democratic reform.

Sadly, the Task Force expended too much effort on proposals aimed at convincing the Cuban establishment of the merits of Western democracy, capitalism, and culture. Instead, we should be developing proposals for ways in which the United States can do in Cuba what it did in Central Europe—support those who are working to promote democracy and create a free society within the decaying shell of Castro's totalitarian system.

Marc A. Thiessen

TASK FORCE MEMBERS

ALLEN R. ADLER is a private investor in the securities markets
and the communications/media industry. In addition, he is a
Trustee of the Simon Wiesenthal Center, the World Policy
Institute, and New York's Lenox Hill Neighborhood House,
among other nonprofit activities, such as the New York Council of Human Rights Watch and the Rockefeller University
Council.

BERNARD W. ARONSON served as Assistant Secretary of State
for Inter-American Affairs from 1989 to 1993. Prior to leaving his post, Mr. Aronson was awarded the State Department's
highest civilian honor, the Distinguished Service Award. He
currently serves as Chairman and Partner of ACON Investments L.L.C., which manages Newbridge Andean Partners
L.P., a private equity fund that makes direct investments in
Latin American companies, primarily in the Andean region.

MARIO L. BAEZA is Chairman & CEO of TCW/Latin America Partners, L.L.C. and various related entities. He is the former President of Wasserstein Perella International, Ltd., and
a former Associate Partner in the international law firm of
Debevoise & Plimpton. Mr. Baeza is a member of the Board
of Directors of the Council on Foreign Relations and of several other nonprofit and for-profit institutions.

TED GALEN CARPENTER is Vice President for Defense and
Foreign Policy Studies at the Cato Institute in Washington,
D.C., and is the author or editor of 12 books on international affairs and a member of the editorial board of the *Journal
of Strategic Studies*.

ALBERTO R. COLL, Dean of the Center for Naval Warfare
Studies at the U.S. Naval War College, served as Principal

Deputy Assistant Secretary of Defense (Special Operations and Low-Intensity Conflict) in the Bush administration. Mr. Coll is the author of several books and numerous articles in the fields of international relations, national security affairs, and U.S. policy toward Latin America.

RODOLFO O. DE LA GARZA is Vice President of the Tomás Rivera Policy Institute and Mike Hogg Professor of Community Affairs in the Department of Government at the University of Texas at Austin, and a specialist in ethnic politics. He is a member of the Council on Foreign Relations, the Pacific Council on International Policy, the Overseas Development Council, and the Hispanic Council on International Affairs.

MARIA DE LOURDES DUKE is President and Founder of Fundacíon Amistad, a nonprofit organization that works to increase awareness of Cuban history, culture, and society. Mrs. Duke has also been the Executive Vice President of the Harbor for Boys and Girls for the past 20 years. She serves on the Board of Directors of the Child Society Center at New York University, the Women's Commission for Refugee Women and Children, and Americans for Humanitarian Trade with Cuba. Mrs. Duke also serves on the Advisory Board for Medical Education Cooperation with Cuba (MEDICC).

MARK FALCOFF is a Resident Scholar at the American Enterprise Institute for Public Policy Research and author of many books and articles on Latin America. He served on the Senate Foreign Relations Committee in the 99ᵗʰ Congress and has been a Visiting Fellow at both the Hoover Institution and the Council on Foreign Relations.

DANIEL W. FISK is Deputy Director of the Kathryn and Shelby Cullom Davis Institute for International Studies at the Heritage Foundation, Washington, D.C. He formerly served on the senior staffs of the U.S. Senate Committee on Foreign Relations and the former U.S. House of Representatives Committee on Foreign Affairs, and in positions at the White House and in the Departments of State and Defense.

ALAN H. FLEISCHMANN is Chief of Staff to Maryland Lt. Governor Kathleen Kennedy Townsend, and was formerly Staff Director of the Subcommittee on the Western Hemisphere for the former U.S. House of Representatives Committee on Foreign Affairs (International Relations). Prior to that, he served as a Vice-President at Latcorp, Inc. and at Chase Manhattan Bank. He is on the Board of Directors of OFFITBank, a New York–based private bank.

CRAIG FULLER is President and Chief Executive Officer of the National Association of Chain Drug Stores. Previously, he was Chairman of Global Board Services and Managing Director of Korn/Ferry International, Vice Chairman of Burson-Marsteller, Senior Vice President for Corporate Affairs at Phillip Morris, and President of Hill & Knowlton. He also served for eight years in the White House during the Reagan administration.

PETER HAKIM is President of the Inter-American Dialogue. He authors a regular column for the *Christian Science Monitor* on Western Hemisphere relations and on political and economic developments in Latin America and the Caribbean. He serves on boards and advisory committees for the World Bank, the Inter-American Development Bank, the State Department, Human Rights Watch, the International Center for Research on Women, and Carnegie Endowment for International Peace.

GARY HUFBAUER is Reginald Jones Scholar at the Institute for International Economics starting in 1992. Dr. Hufbauer served as the Maurice R. Greenberg Chair and Director of Studies at the Council on Foreign Relations (1997–98). He was previously Professor of International Financial Diplomacy and Deputy Assistant Secretary at the Treasury Department.

ADRIAN KARATNYCKY is President of Freedom House, a nonpartisan, nonprofit organization that promotes democracy, civil society, and the rule of law, and monitors democratic change, political rights, and civil liberties throughout the world. He coordinates *Freedom in the World*, the Annual Survey of Political Rights and Civil Liberties.

WENDY W. LUERS, President and founder of The Foundation for a Civil Society, New York, is also the founder, consultant, and Steering Committee member of the Project on Justice in Times of Transition, an inter-faculty conflict resolution project at Harvard University.

JAY MAZUR, President of the Union of Needletrades, Industrial and Textile Employees (UNITE), is a member of the Executive Council of the AFL-CIO and chairs its International Relations Committee. He is Chairman of the Amalgamated Bank of New York and a member of the Council on Foreign Relations and the Trilateral Commission.

PHILIP PETERS is Vice President of the Lexington Institute, where he publishes research and analysis of Cuba's economy and U.S. policy. He served in the State Department during the Reagan and Bush administrations.

SUSAN KAUFMAN PURCELL is Vice President of the Americas Society in New York City. She was Senior Fellow and Director of the Latin American Project at the Council on Foreign Relations (1981–88). She also served at the U.S. State Department's Policy Planning Staff, with responsibility for Latin America and the Caribbean (1980–81).

PETER W. RODMAN, Director of National Security Programs at The Nixon Center, has served as a Deputy Assistant to the President for National Security Affairs and as Director of the State Department Policy Planning Staff. He is on the Boards of Freedom House and of the World Affairs Council of Washington, D.C.

WILLIAM D. ROGERS is Senior Partner at Arnold & Porter and also Vice Chair at Kissinger Associates. Mr. Rogers was formerly Assistant Secretary of State for Inter-American Affairs and Under Secretary of State for International Economic Affairs.

MICHO FERNANDEZ SPRING is a partner at BSMG Worldwide and was formerly Deputy Mayor of Boston. In addition, she serves as Co-Chair of Catholic Charities Caritas Cubana Committee and on the Boards of Brigham and Women's Hospital and Partners Health Care and Catholic Charities, and is a Director at Citizens Bank of Massachusetts.

ALEXANDER F. WATSON, Vice President for International Conservation at the Nature Conservancy in Arlington, Virginia, was a career Foreign Service Officer for more than 30 years. He completed his service as Ambassador to Peru, Deputy Permanent Representative to the United Nations, and Assistant Secretary of State for Inter-American Affairs. He also served as President of the Pan American Development Foundation.

MARIA C. WERLAU is President and founder of Orbis International S.A., specializing in diverse advisory services and international relocation in Latin America. Formerly a Second Vice President at Chase Manhattan Bank, she has extensively written on economic issues, U.S.-Cuba policy, and human rights.

TASK FORCE OBSERVERS

FULTON T. ARMSTRONG has been the National Intelligence Officer for Latin America since June 2000. Previously he served as Chief of Staff of the Directorate of Central Intelligence Crime and Narcotics Center; two terms as a Director for Inter-American Affairs at the National Security Council (1995–97 and 1998–99); and as Deputy National Intelligence Officer for Latin America (1997–98). Before that, he held various analytical and policy positions, including political-economic officer at the U.S. Interests Section in Havana.

NADINE BERG is a Legislative Assistant for Congressman José E. Serrano.

JEFFREY DELAURENTIS is Chief of the Political/Economic Section of the U.S. Interests Section in Havana, Cuba. A career Foreign Service Officer since 1991, he had an earlier posting in Havana and has also served at the U.S. Mission to the United Nations, the National Security Council (Director for Inter-American Affairs focusing on Cuba), and as Executive Assistant to the Acting Assistant Secretary for Western Hemisphere Affairs.

PAULA J. DOBRANSKY, Vice President and Director of the Washington Office of the Council on Foreign Relations, was formerly Associate Director for Policy and Programs at the United States Information Agency, Deputy Assistant Secretary of State for Human Rights and Humanitarian Affairs, and Director of European and Soviet Affairs at the National Security Council.

EDWARD H. EDENS IV has been a Professional Staff Member for the Senate Armed Services Committee since January

1999. Previously he served as Deputy Staff Director for the Senate Committee on Rules and Administration (1995–99) and as a member of Senator John Warner's (R-Va.) personal staff (1986–95).

BOB FILIPPONE is the National Security Adviser to Senator Bob Graham (D-Fla.). Prior to joining Senator Graham's staff, he worked in the Office of the Secretary of Defense and the Bureau of Intelligence and Research at the Department of State.

J. BRENT GIBADLO was Legislative Assistant in the office of Congressman Mark Sanford (R-S.C.).

LEE H. HAMILTON is Director of the Woodrow Wilson International Center for Scholars. Previously, Mr. Hamilton served as a U.S. Congressman from Indiana for 34 years. During his tenure he served in many capacities as a member of the former Committee on Foreign Affairs (International Relations) and Chairman of the Joint Economic Committee, Permanent Select Committee on Intelligence, Joint Committee on the Organization of Congress, and Select Committee to Investigate Covert Arms Transactions with Iran.

CARYN HOLLIS is a Director for Inter-American Affairs, National Security Council. Ms. Hollis is on a rotational assignment from the Office of the Secretary of Defense, where she served as the Acting Principal Director of the Inter-American Region, from May until December 1999.

ALAN HOWARD is a writer and also assistant to the president of UNITE. He has written about U.S.-Latin American relations for the *New York Times Magazine, The Nation*, and public television.

BERNARD CARDINAL LAW has been Archbishop of Boston since 1984 and a member of numerous councils and congregations on migration, culture, and spiritual development. The Archbishop has served on the Boards of Trustees of the

Catholic University of America and the National Shrine of the Immaculate Conception. He has served other congregations in Mississippi and Missouri.

GORDON LEDERMAN is a member of Arnold & Porter's Public Policy/Legislative Group and practices in the fields of government relations (focusing on national security issues), litigation, and international arbitration. Mr. Lederman authored *Reorganizing the Joint Chiefs of Staff: The Goldwater-Nichols Act of 1986.*

TAUNYA MCLARTY is Legislative Counsel to Senator John Ashcroft (R-Mo.) and has been pivotal in drafting and pushing through Congress legislative initiatives on trade, most recently a proposal to lift the embargo on agricultural and medical exports to five countries.

ROBERT R. NEAL, Senior Legislative Assistant in the office of Congressman George R. Nethercutt Jr. (R-Wash.), worked on recent legislation to lift food and medicine sanctions on Cuba, along with similar legislation that blocked the imposition of sanctions on Pakistan in 1998.

BRETT W. O'BRIEN is Senior Foreign and Defense Policy Adviser to Democratic Leader Rep. Richard A. Gephardt (D-Mo.). Mr. O'Brien also served as Foreign and Defense Policy Adviser for U.S. Senate Majority Leader George J. Mitchell (D-Me.).

JANICE O'CONNELL has been a Professional Staff Member of the U.S. Senate Foreign Relations Committee for 23 years and is Senior Foreign Policy Assistant to Senator Christopher J. Dodd (D-Conn.).

THOMAS E. QUIGLEY is Policy Adviser for Latin American and Caribbean Affairs at the Catholic Bishops' Conference. He has assisted in the drafting of all statements of the U.S. bishops on Cuba, and has written and spoken widely on church relations in Cuba, most notably around the papal visit of 1998.

CHARLES SHAPIRO, the Coordinator for Cuban Affairs at the U.S. Department of State, is a career Foreign Service Officer who has spent the majority of his career at posts in Latin America and the Caribbean or working on related issues in Washington.

SUSAN SNYDER is the Special Assistant to Ambassador Wendy Sherman, Counselor of the Department of State. Ms. Snyder's portfolio includes Cuba.

MARC A. THIESSEN is Press Spokesman of the U.S. Senate Foreign Relations Committee.

APPENDIX

The following is excerpted from the 1999 Independent Task Force Report, U.S.-Cuban Relations in the 21st Century *(New York: Council on Foreign Relations, 1999).*

RECOMMENDATIONS

BASKET ONE: THE CUBAN AMERICAN COMMUNITY

Cuban American remittances to friends, families, and churches in Cuba are estimated by various sources at between $400 million and $800 million annually. However measured, this is the island's largest single source of hard currency. Although it is perfectly normal for developing countries to receive remittances, in the Cuban political context, the dependence on U.S. dollars sent home by Cuban Americans is a humiliating badge of failure. Cuba has become a charity case, dependent on handouts from those it has persecuted, oppressed, or driven away by poverty.

Some voices in the United States argue that, by enhancing hard-currency holdings in Cuba, remittances prop up the current regime and prolong the island's agony. This argument is not without merit, but, on balance, we disagree. First, we share a basic moral and humanitarian concern over easing the suffering of Cuba's people. Moreover, the success of the Cuban American community is one of the most powerful factors in promoting change in Cuba. The transfers of money, goods, and medical supplies from Cuban Americans to friends, family, and religious communities in Cuba are helping create a new group of Cubans who no longer depend on the state for their means of survival.

Remittances from Cuban Americans help create small businesses in Cuba and allow hundreds of thousands of Cubans to improve their lives independent of government control. Furthermore, Cuban Americans will play an important role in the construction of a postcommunist Cuba. Their national and global contacts, understanding of market economies, and professional skills will give them a vital role as a bridge between the United States and Cuba when Cuba rejoins the democratic community.

Cuban American Community Recommendations

1. End Restrictions on Humanitarian Visits. We recommend an end to all restrictions on the number of humanitarian visits that Cuban Americans are permitted to make each year. The federal government should not be the judge of how often Cuban Americans, or any other Americans, need to visit relatives living abroad.

2. Raise the Ceiling on Remittances. Under current regulations, only Cuban Americans are permitted to send up to $1,200 per year to family members on the island. We recommend that the ceiling on annual remittances be increased to $10,000 per household and that all U.S. residents with family members living in Cuba should be permitted to send remittances to their family members at this level on a trial basis for 18 months. This policy should continue if the executive, in consultation with Congress, concludes at the trial period's end that the Cuban regime has not enacted tax or other regulatory policies to siphon off a significant portion of these funds, and that this policy furthers the foreign policy interests of the United States.

3. Allow Retirement to Cuba for Cuban Americans. We recommend that retired and/or disabled Cuban Americans be allowed to return to Cuba if they choose, collecting Social Security and other pension benefits to which they are entitled in the United States, and be granted corresponding banking facilities.

4. Promote Family Reunification. Many members of the Cuban American community are concerned about the difficulty their family members in Cuba encounter in getting U.S. visas for family visits. While commending the efforts of the overworked consular staff in Havana, we believe it is important that Cuban Americans receive and be seen to receive fair and courteous treatment. We recommend that the State Department and Immigration and Naturalization Service (INS) make every effort in processing requests at the U.S. Interests Section in Havana to insure that Cuban citizens wishing to visit family members in the United States face no higher hurdle in obtaining visas than that faced by family members in other countries wishing to visit relatives in this country. We recommend that State Department and INS officials meet regularly with representatives of the Cuban American commu-

nity to discuss ways to expedite the determination of eligibility for family visits to the United States. Later in this report, we recommend an expansion of U.S. consular services in Cuba.

5. Restore Direct Mail Service. The 1992 Cuban Democracy Act grants the president the authority to authorize direct mail service between the United States and Cuba. We recommend that representatives of the U.S. and Cuban postal services meet to begin restoring direct mail service between the two countries.

BASKET TWO: THE OPEN DOOR

Since the passage of the 1992 Cuban Democracy Act, U.S. law has recognized that spreading accurate and fair information about the outside world in Cuba is an important goal of American foreign policy. The lack of information about events in Cuba has also enabled the Cuban regime to persecute its own people with little fear that foreigners will come to their support—or, in some cases, even know what the Cuban government is doing. Whether through Radio Martí, restoring direct telephone service, or promoting cultural and academic exchanges, the United States has consistently sought to increase the access of Cubans to news and information from abroad.

We believe the time has come to significantly upgrade and intensify these efforts. The Cuban people are hungry for American and world culture, for contacts with scholars and artists from other countries, for opportunities to study abroad, for new ideas and fresh perspectives. U.S. policy should encourage these exchanges and encounters through every available measure.

Open Door Recommendations

1. Facilitate Targeted Travel. Despite bureaucratic obstacles erected by both governments, the exchange of ideas remains one of the most promising areas for genuinely fruitful people-to-people contact. Since 1995, the United States has significantly cut the red tape surrounding academic exchanges. We commend that trend and urge the further reduction of restrictions on academic (undergraduate, graduate, and postgraduate) and other exchanges. We recommend that, following a one-time application, the Office of Foreign Assets Control (OFAC) grant a "permanent specific license" to all Americans with a demonstrable professional or other serious interest in traveling to Cuba for the pur-

pose of engaging in academic, scientific, environmental, health, cultural, athletic, religious, or other activities. The presumption would be that these applications would normally and routinely receive approval.[2]

In 1994, Congress passed a Sense of Congress resolution stating that "the president should not restrict travel or exchanges for informational, educational, religious, cultural or humanitarian purposes or for public performances or exhibitions between the United States and any other country." At the same time, congressional policy toward Cuba has increasingly focused on opening opportunities for meaningful encounters between American and Cuban citizens. Thus, we recommend that the OFAC grant easily renewable multiple-entry special licenses to travel agencies and nongovernmental organizations for structured travel programs available to groups and individuals for the purposes enumerated by Congress. Individual participants in such travel would visit Cuba under the organizing agency's license.

This recommendation is formulated to facilitate a more open relationship between Cubans and Americans, not to support a Cuban tourism industry currently built on a system that prevents foreign employers from hiring and paying workers fairly and directly and denies Cuban citizens access to facilities designated exclusively or foreigners. When and if employers are able to hire and pay their workers directly, and when the system of "apartheid tourism" ends, we recommend that the United States consider permitting leisure travel.

2. **Allow More Private Visits of Certain Cuban Officials to the United States.** The United States currently denies visas for travel to the United States by Cuban officials who rank at the ministerial level and by the 500 deputies of the National Assembly of People's Power. Because of the positions they now hold and may assume in the future, many such individuals are among those we believe should have the opportunity to interact with Americans, to experience our system directly, and to witness the vigor and openness of our own public policy debate. We recommend that the United States lift its blanket ban on travel to the United

---

[2]Current regulations require all individuals wishing to travel to Cuba (with the exception of journalists who may travel without government preclearance under a "general license") to apply for a "specific license," for which applicants must demonstrate a preestablished legitimate professional or research interest in Cuba. Persons traveling under a "general license" to Cuba are not required to clear their plans with the U.S. government in advance. They are, however, required to certify at reentry to the United States that their travel and activities in Cuba conformed to the purposes for which the licenses are granted; making false statements a violation of federal law.

States by deputies of the National Assembly and Cuban cabinet ministers, exercising a presumption of approval for applications from these officials for travel to the United States, except for those identified by the State Department who are credibly believed to have directly and personally participated in or ordered grave acts of repression that violate international law, or who represent a legitimate security concern to the United States. In making this recommendation we seek to encourage nongovernmental and private contacts such as those sponsored by U.S. academic institutions. We recognize that this recommendation risks greater penetration of the United States by Cuban intelligence agencies. We have confidence in the ability of U.S. national security agencies to guard against this threat, and we believe that the gains far outweigh the risks. Nevertheless, this danger must be carefully watched and adjustments in this policy calibrated accordingly.

3. Facilitate Cultural Collaboration and Performances by Americans in Cuba and by Cubans in the United States. Since the passage of the 1992 Cuban Democracy Act, there has been a significant increase in the number of Cuban artists, actors, and musicians traveling to the United States. Unfortunately, fewer U.S. performers have traveled to Cuba. These exchanges and activities are vital to any strategy to end the cultural isolation of the Cuban people. Through simplified visa and license procedures and other mechanisms, the U.S. government should encourage an increase in these programs. We applaud efforts to date to support such initiatives and recommend further that the United States encourage collaboration between American and Cuban artists and allow transactions for the creation of new cultural and/or artistic products. Cuban artists performing in the United States today are allowed to receive only modest per diem payments to cover living expenses. We recommend that Cuban artists performing in the United States be allowed to receive freely negotiated fees from their American hosts. Similarly, American artists performing in Cuba should be eligible to be paid for their work at reasonable negotiated rates.

4. Protect and Share Intellectual Property. Currently, Cuba systematically pirates significant amounts of U.S. cultural and intellectual property, ranging from Hollywood movies broadcast on Cuban television to computer software used throughout the island. Cuba refuses to consider paying for this illegal use of intellectual property, citing the U.S. embargo as an excuse. This creates an awkward situation for the United States. On the one hand, our interest in opening Cuba to outside influences leads us to encourage and even facilitate Cuba's access to U.S.

and other foreign films, cultural materials, and political and economic literature. On the other hand, the U.S. government cannot condone theft from U.S. citizens and corporations. Furthermore, we must ensure that Cuba does not become an international center for the illegal production and redistribution of pirated intellectual property. We therefore propose that the United States allow and encourage U.S. companies and artists to guarantee and protect their trademarks and copyrights and to negotiate permission for Cuba to use their products. We recommend that the U.S. government license and approve these transactions and authorize companies to spend funds obtained through these settlements for filming, recording, translation, or other legitimate cultural activities in Cuba. Likewise, we encourage both governments to regularize and comply with domestic and international trademark and copyright protection regimes.

5. Pioneer "Windows on the World." Successful transitions to multiparty systems and market and mixed market economies in eastern Europe, Spain, Portugal, and Latin America may offer constructive guideposts to help Cuba's transition occur in as benign a manner as possible. To that end, the United States should pioneer the creation of a merit-based program for Cubans to study in American universities and technical training institutes. The program should also include sending professionals with technical expertise to advise Cuba in the development of institutional mechanisms that support the emergence of small businesses and private farms. In addition, we recommend that the United States Information Agency (USIA) invite Cuban government officials (except those excluded as defined in Basket Two, Item Two) and scholars for its programs that bring foreign citizens to meet with their peers in and out of government in the United States.

We further recommend that funds be made available from various public and independent sources, such as the National Endowment for the Arts, the National Endowment for Humanities, the National Endowment for Democracy, the Fulbright scholarship program, and from private foundations for university and other programs to support national, regional, and bilateral research activities involving Cuba. This includes support for new acquisitions by Cuban libraries. In addition, we recommend that the United States encourage and facilitate direct funding of in-country activities by private foundations so that their grant-making activities can include direct support to Cuban research institutions and community organizations. We recommend that the U.S. government consult with foundation officers and others with expertise in this field to determine a fair and feasible approach. We note with concern that some academic and other nongovernmental institutions, citing pressure from the Cuban government, have barred Cuban Americans from participating in existing exchange programs. Discrimination based on ethnicity or place of origin is a violation of U.S. civil rights laws. All organizations participating in exchanges or other activities with Cuba should state clearly that in compliance with U.S. law, they will not discriminate against participants based on age, race, gender, or national origin.

6. Permit Direct Commercial Flights. We recommend that the OFAC authorize and license direct commercial flights to Cuba. Current regulations authorize daily direct charter flights between Miami and Havana. It is not in the U.S. national interest that non-U.S. carriers capture the entire market of expanding travel to and from Cuba. We therefore recommend that American commercial airlines begin to open routes to Havana and perhaps other Cuban cities not only from Miami but from other major cities and hubs. We recommend also that the United States and Cuba negotiate a civil aviation agreement to this end.

7. Amend Spending Limits. Current regulations limit licensed travelers to Cuba to spending no more than $100 per day, plus transportation and expenses for the acquisition of informational materials, including artwork. We recommend that the OFAC impose this limit only on spending in state-owned enterprises and joint ventures.

8. Expand Diplomatic and Consular Services. The recommendations in this report will greatly increase demands on the U.S. Interests Section in Cuba. Current U.S. consular services in Cuba should not be limited to Havana. We recommend that the United States open a subsection of its Havana consular office in Santiago de Cuba, a step that will also increase our ability to fill the quota of 5,000 slots available for Cuban political refugees each year. We recommend that the United States negotiate a reciprocal agreement with Cuba that will allow each country to expand its consular services to accommodate increased contact between citizens of both countries.

9. Demand Reciprocity in Limitations on Activities by U.S. and Cuban Diplomats. At present, an imbalance exists wherein American diplomats in Havana are denied access to government offices, the courts, the National Assembly, the University, and virtually all official Cuban facilities other than the Ministry of Foreign Relations. The same is not the case in Washington, where Cuban diplomats freely walk the halls of Congress, meet with elected representatives, speak at universities, and otherwise have access to a fairly wide range of American governmen-

tal and nongovernmental representatives. We recommend that the United States and Cuba discuss a reciprocal widening of the areas of permitted activities for diplomats in both countries.

BASKET THREE: HUMANITARIAN AID

The 1992 Cuban Democracy Act established regulations addressing the humanitarian needs of the Cuban population. Since then, the economic crisis has worsened. This basket of recommendations includes humanitarian measures that will help relieve the suffering of the Cuban people today while building the basis for a better relationship between Cuba and the United States in the future.

Humanitarian Aid Recommendations

1. Institute "Cash and Carry" for Foods and Medicines. We applaud the intention behind recent efforts in the Congress and the executive branch to facilitate the increased delivery of humanitarian aid to Cuba. Recognizing that a consensus is emerging to extend humanitarian aid to benefit the Cuban people directly, we recommend that the president accelerate and facilitate this process by eliminating all licensing with respect to donation and sales of food, medicines, and medical products to nongovernmental and humanitarian institutions such as hospitals, which are nominally state-run but are not primarily instruments of repression, while authorizing all necessary financial transactions for cash payments on a noncredit basis. We recommend that the State Department issue a specific list of repressive institutions that are to be excluded as potential aid recipients or buyers.[3] To further facilitate donations and sales of food, medicines, and medical products, we recommend that the United States issue licenses to U.S. private voluntary and religious organizations, nongovernmental organizations, and businesses to operate distribution centers in Cuba.

---

[3]For instance, identifying the Ministry of Interior as an excluded institution would have the effect of excluding fire departments throughout the island, which in our view are legitimate potential recipients of aid or purchasers of food and medicine. On the other hand, the Ministry of Interior is also responsible for running the Bureau of Prisons, an agency that international human rights groups regularly charge with engaging in repressive activities. Thus, in carrying out this recommendation, the State Department should focus sanctions as specifically as possible on those agencies that are actually responsible for repressive activities.

2. Promote People-to-People Aid. We support American engagement with a wide range of civil institutions, particularly those in the private sector; e.g., the emerging church-run medical clinics and humanitarian institutions such as hospitals, which are nominally state-run but are not primarily instruments of repression. With the support and encouragement of the Congress, the administration has significantly widened the opening for Americans to launch humanitarian, people-to-people programs in Cuba. We encourage American local governments and nongovernmental organizations to "adopt" their Cuban counterparts, whether through church, hospital, school, environmental, or university programs. The United States should eliminate the need for licenses for humanitarian donations and shipments, including material aid and cash, and should grant a general license for related travel. We recommend that the United States impose no limit on the amount of material donations under such programs, while requiring a license for cash donations above $10,000 per year by any one American institution to its Cuban counterpart—with the exception of private foundations, for which we recommend waiving that limit and permitting the grant-making bodies to use their own institutional criteria to determine in-country funding limits. In the same spirit as that which underlies the Basket One recommendation regarding family remittances, we recommend the United States permit American families to adopt and send remittances to Cuban families of up to $10,000 per year.

3. Allow Cuban Americans to Claim Relatives as Dependents. Currently American citizens with dependent relatives living in Canada and Mexico can claim them as dependents for federal income tax purposes if they meet the other relevant IRS requirements. We recommend an amendment to U.S. tax laws so that American taxpayers with dependents who are residents of Cuba can also claim this deduction.

4. Provide Benefits for Families of Prisoners of Conscience. Under current law, the president may extend humanitarian assistance to victims of political repression and their families in Cuba. We recommend that the United States encourage our European and Latin American allies to join with us to provide support and assistance to family members who, because of their imprisoned relatives' peaceful political activities, may find themselves denied access to jobs by Cuban authorities or who have lost the wages of an imprisoned spouse or parent. If it is not possible to deliver the funds to affected families in Cuba today, we recommend that the funds be paid into interest-bearing accounts in the United States and elsewhere, free of all tax, to accumulate until such time as the intended recipients can collect.

Appendix

BASKET FOUR: THE PRIVATE SECTOR

Private-sector, for-profit business activity in Cuba by U.S. individuals and corporations raises a number of difficult issues. To take one example, Cuban labor laws currently require foreign investors to contract Cuban workers indirectly through the Ministry of Labor and Social Security, a violation of internationally recognized labor rights. Although there are some minor exceptions to the rule, the overall result of these requirements is that the foreign investor pays several hundred dollars per month per worker, but the worker receives no more than a few dollars per month. By allowing the Cuban state to control which Cubans have access to coveted jobs with foreign investors, the system reinforces the Cuban regime's control over the lives of the Cuban people.

Until a complete settlement of the claims resulting from nationalization of private property in Cuba is reached, U.S. investors in Cuba could conceivably end up buying or profiting from nationalized property and find their titles or earnings challenged under international law by the original owners. Many trademark and other intellectual property problems involve the two countries. Cuba's insistence that most foreign investment take the form of joint ventures in which the Cuban government often retains a controlling interest is another serious problem, as is the incompatibility of Cuba's legal and financial arrangements with U.S. trade policy.

In formulating our recommendations about private U.S. business in Cuba, we once again try to walk a middle way. These recommendations open a door for Cuba progressively to escape some of the consequences of the embargo—to the extent that the Cuban government gives Cubans the right to own and operate their own enterprises, allows foreign companies to hire Cubans directly, and begins to respect basic internationally recognized labor rights. The recommendations will make clear to the Cuban people (as well as to other countries) that the chief obstacle to Cuba's economic progress is not U.S. policy but the Cuban government's hostility toward private property and independent business, its control of the economy and investment, its persistent appropriation of the lion's share of the wages of working Cubans, and its unwillingness to allow companies to pay fair wages to their employees or permit them to engage in free collective bargaining.

PRIVATE SECTOR RECOMMENDATIONS

1. Begin Licensing Some American Business Activity. We recommend that four limited categories of American businesses receive licenses to oper-

ate in Cuba. The first category—already eligible for licensing—can generally be described as newsgathering or the procurement of informational material. The second category relates to supporting licensed travel, including transportation to and from Cuba and services to assist the private sector, such as *paladares* and bed and breakfasts, in capturing the business resulting from increased licensed travel. (Examples of this type of business are guides and Internet registries that provide information for foreign visitors about private restaurants, bed and breakfasts, car services, and other private services available in Cuba.) The third category includes activities related to distribution of humanitarian aid and sales. In the fourth category are businesses that facilitate activities related to culture, including the production of new cultural materials, the purchase and sale of artworks and other cultural materials, and the verification of Cuban adherence to intellectual property rights agreements. These four categories, in our judgment, provide such clear benefits that we recommend the U.S. government begin licensing private businesses to operate in all these fields, each of which involves primarily activities that support objectives clearly specified in U.S. law. The U.S. government should routinely license business operations in Cuba restricted to these four areas and allow the transactions and support services necessary to conduct them.

2. Condition Additional American Business Activity. Beyond these limited areas, a number of groups have looked at how to structure U.S. business relations in Cuba without reinforcing the status quo. One of the best known is a set of guidelines known as the Arcos Principles. Drawing from these and similar efforts such as the Sullivan Principles in South Africa and the MacBride Principles in Northern Ireland, we recommend that American businesses demonstrate that they can satisfy three core conditions before being licensed to invest in Cuba for activities beyond the four specified above: the ability to hire and pay Cuban workers directly and not through a government agency; a pledge by the company to respect workers' internationally recognized rights of free association; and a pledge by the company not to discriminate against Cuban citizens in the provision of goods and services. (The final condition is designed to counter the practice of "tourism apartheid" in which certain foreign-owned and -operated facilities do not allow Cuban citizens to use their facilities, even when they have the money to pay.) We would also encourage U.S. investors—indeed, all foreign investors in Cuba—to provide reading rooms, classes, Internet access, and other on-site facilities so that their employees can enjoy wider access to the world. If Cuba should change its labor laws to make compliance with these principles

easier, it would then become much easier for U.S. companies to invest. For a specific business license to be approved, however, it is enough for a particular company to demonstrate that it can satisfy the three criteria listed above.

If and when Cuban law is changed to facilitate compliance with the core principles outlined above, or if Cuban authorities begin to grant exemptions and waivers on a routine basis, we would recommend that Congress and the executive consider broader application of such licensing. In all cases, licensing a business to operate under these provisions would in no way reduce the risk of incurring Helms-Burton penalties for trafficking in confiscated property.

BASKET FIVE: THE NATIONAL INTEREST

National Interest Recommendations

1. Conduct Military-to-Military Confidence-Building Measures. Both Presidents Bush and Clinton have stated that the United States has no aggressive intentions toward Cuba, and the Pentagon has concluded that Cuba poses no significant national security threat to the United States. We believe, therefore, that it is in our national interest to promote greater ties and cooperation with the Cuban military. We believe the more confident the Cuban military is that the United States will not take military advantage of a political or economic opening, the more likely it is that elements of the Cuban Armed Forces will tolerate or support such an opening and the less justifiable it will be to divert public resources from social needs to maintaining a defense force far beyond the legitimate needs of the nation. We believe this process should proceed on a step-by-step basis with many of the initial contacts through civilian agencies, both governmental and nongovernmental. We also believe it would be useful for the United States to encourage an opening of relations between militaries in other nations that have carried out successful transitions from communist regimes to democratic societies, such as those in eastern Europe and, where appropriate, in Latin America. We also recommend that the Pentagon and State Department initiate conversations with the Cuban Armed Forces and others to reduce tensions, promote mutual confidence-building measures, and lay the basis for the improvement of relations in the future should Cuba move toward a democratic transition.

2. Probe Areas for Counternarcotics Cooperation. Cuba sits at the center of a substantial drug trade in the Caribbean Basin. Its neighbor to the east, Haiti, has recently emerged as a major port for cocaine transit from South America to the United States. Despite the outstanding indictments against some Cuban officials for alleged drug trafficking, the Cuban state has both the geographical and the institutional resources to help America fight the war on drugs if the Cuban regime chooses to do so. In recent years, the United States and Cuba have cooperated on a limited case-by-case basis in counternarcotics efforts in the Caribbean Basin. We recommend that the appropriate U.S. government agencies test Cuba's willingness to take serious steps to demonstrate its good faith in furthering cooperation in the counternarcotics arena, while protecting the confidentiality of U.S. intelligence sources and methods. We note that Cuba still harbors individuals indicted in the United States on serious drug trafficking charges. Clearly, limited cooperation in this area will depend on a demonstrated willingness by the Cuban government to address this issue seriously.

3. Institute Routine Executive Branch Consultations with Congress and Others on Cuba Policy. We recommend continued and enhanced bipartisan consultations by the executive branch with Congress and with a broad range of leaders representing political, social, and economic groups in the Cuban American, humanitarian, religious, academic, and cultural communities. As we have seen in U.S. policy toward Central America, and throughout most of the post–Cold War era, a bipartisan consensus between Congress and the executive is a precondition for sustaining a long-term, successful U.S. foreign policy initiative.

4. Form a Working Group on the 21st Century. When people in both the United States and Cuba talk about the future relationship between the two countries, they often speak of the "normalization of relations." In fact, the United States and Cuba have not had "normal" relations since the United States intervened to end Spanish rule in 1898. Since the current Cuban regime came to power in 1959, it has employed a formidable propaganda machine to cloak Cuban nationalism in a banner of anti-American rhetoric. Cuban schoolchildren are taught to view the Cuban revolution as the only legitimate guarantor of national sovereignty and to regard the United States as a constant threat to Cuba's independence. However opposed the United States has been and remains to the present Cuban government, the American people have no interest in intruding upon Cuba's sovereignty, independence, or national identity. As Cuba inaugurates its second century of independence, we recommend that the Council on Foreign Relations or another similar private

Appendix

institution convene a binational working group of scholars, policy analysts, and others to begin working out an agenda for a new relationship between the United States and Cuba in the 21st century, analyzing a range of complex bilateral and regional issues, including the resolution of outstanding property claims; the status of the U.S. military base at Guantánamo Bay; the implications for the Western Hemisphere of the restoration of a Cuban sugar quota; the impact on the Caribbean economy of resuming normal bilateral trade relations; Cuban participation in the Caribbean Basin Initiative (CBI) and the Free Trade Area of the Americas (FTAA); prospects for Cuba's reentry into the Organization of American States (OAS); and the integration of Cuba into the international financial system.

FOLLOW-UP STEPS

These proposals represent a beginning of what we hope will become a growing bipartisan policy toward Cuba. We believe that responsible officials and interested individuals and groups should monitor the effect of these recommendations, should they be implemented, and after a reasonable period of time assess whether changes, modifications, and additional steps are warranted.

OTHER REPORTS OF INDEPENDENT TASK FORCES SPONSORED BY THE COUNCIL ON FOREIGN RELATIONS

---

*Available from Brookings Institution Press. To order, call 1-800-275-1447.
†Available on the Council on Foreign Relations website at www.cfr.org.